FOR THE MANY
NOT THE FEW

CONTENTS

FOREWORD

A big part of being the leader of a political party is that you meet people across the country and hear a wide range of views and ideas about the future. For me, it's been a reminder that our country is a place of dynamic, generous and creative people with massive potential.

But I've also heard something far less positive, something which motivates us in the Labour Party to work for the kind of real change set out in this manifesto. It is a growing sense of anxiety and frustration.

Faced with falling living standards, growing job insecurity and shrinking public services, people are under increasing strain. Young people are held back by debt and the cost of housing. Whole families are being held back from the life they have worked towards.

I'm constantly told of these pressures in the workplace. Faced with constant cuts and interference, our police, nurses, doctors, teachers and council staff are held back from delivering the public services they signed up to.

Workers are held back by falling real pay and job security. Our entrepreneurs and managers are being held back from growing their business. If you are increasingly asked to do more with less, then you are not alone.

Every election is a choice. What makes this election different is that the choice is starker than ever before. You can choose more of the same: the rich getting richer, more children in poverty, our NHS failing and our schools and social care in crisis. Or you can vote for the party that has a plan to change all of this – The Labour Party.

Britain is the fifth richest country in the world. But that means little when many people don't share in that wealth. Many feel the system is rigged against them. And this manifesto sets out exactly what can be done about it.

Britain needs to negotiate a Brexit deal that puts our economy and living standards first. That won't be achieved by empty slogans and posturing. We cannot put at risk our links with our largest trading partner. Instead we need a jobs-first Brexit that allows us to upgrade our economy for the 21st century.

Labour will invest in the cutting-edge jobs and industries of the future that can improve everybody's lives. Which is why this manifesto outlines a fully costed programme to upgrade our economy. From childcare to transport, housing to lifelong learning, Labour understands how a successful economy depends on services that support us all.

So yes, this election is about what sort of country we want to be after Brexit. Is it one where the majority are held back by the sheer struggle of getting by? That isn't the Britain Labour is determined to create.

So let's build a fairer Britain where no one is held back. A country where everybody is able to get on in life, to have security at work and at home, to be decently paid for the work they do, and to live their lives with the dignity they deserve.

Let's build a country where we invest our wealth to give everyone the best chance. That means building the homes we need to rent and buy, keeping our communities safe with more police officers, giving our children's schools the funding they badly need, and restoring the NHS to its place as the envy of the world.

Don't let the Conservatives hold Britain back.

Let's build a Britain that works for the many, not the few.

Jeremy Corbyn

Jeremy Corbyn
Leader of the Labour Party

CHAPTER 01

CREATING AN ECONOMY THAT WORKS FOR ALL

CREATING AN ECONOMY THAT WORKS FOR ALL

Labour's economic strategy is about delivering a fairer, more prosperous society for the many, not just the few.

We will measure our economic success not by the number of billionaires, but by the ability of our people to live richer lives.

Labour understands that the creation of wealth is a collective endeavour between workers, entrepreneurs, investors and government. Each contributes and each must share fairly in the rewards.

This manifesto sets out Labour's plan to upgrade our economy and rewrite the rules of a rigged system, so that our economy really works for the many, and not only the few. Britain is the only major developed economy where earnings have fallen even as growth has returned after the financial crisis. Most working people in Britain today are earning less, after inflation, than they did ten years ago. Too many of us are in low-paid and insecure work. Too many of us fear our children will not enjoy the same opportunities that we have.

Labour will turn this around. We will upgrade our economy, breaking down the barriers that hold too many of us back, and tackling the gender pay gap. Our National Transformation Fund will deliver the investment that every part of Britain needs to meet its potential, overcoming years of neglect. Our industrial strategy will support businesses to create new, high-skilled, high-paid and secure work across the country, in the sectors of the future such as renewables. We will stop our financial system being rigged for the few, turning the power of finance to work for the public good. And we will put small businesses at the centre of our economic strategy.

The growth created by our national investment plan, underpinned by the responsible economic management embodied in our Fiscal Credibility Rule, will create good jobs, drive up living standards and improve the public finances.

It is a plan that will deliver Labour's vision of an economy that works for the many, not just the few – a Britain in which no one is held back.

A FAIR TAXATION SYSTEM

Taxation is what underpins our shared prosperity. All of us, including business, benefit from a healthy, educated and skilled population, with access to basic services and secure housing.

We believe in the social obligation to contribute to a fair taxation scheme for the common good. We will take on the social scourge of tax avoidance through our Tax Transparency and Enforcement Programme, and close down tax loopholes.

But we will not ask ordinary households to pay more. A Labour government will guarantee no rises in income tax for those earning below £80,000 a year, and no increases in personal National Insurance Contributions or the rate of VAT.

Under Labour's plans, 95 per cent of taxpayers will be guaranteed no increase in their income tax contributions, and everyone will be protected from any increase in personal National Insurance contributions and VAT. Only the top 5 per cent of earners will be asked to contribute more in tax to help fund our public services. We renew our pledge not to extend VAT to food, children's clothes, books and newspapers, and public transport fares.

Corporation tax in the UK is the lowest of any major developed economy. Our new settlement with business will ask large corporations to pay a little more while still keeping UK corporation tax among the lowest of the major developed economies. In turn, we will meet the business need for a more skilled workforce with extra corporate tax revenues while contributing to education and skills budgets.

We will protect small businesses by reintroducing the lower small profits rate of corporation tax. We will also exclude small businesses from costly plans to introduce quarterly reporting and take action on late payments.

Labour will give HM Revenue & Customs the resources and skills necessary to clamp down hard on those unscrupulous few individuals and companies who seek to avoid the responsibilities that the rest of us meet.

BALANCING THE BOOKS

Our manifesto is fully costed, with all current spending paid for out of taxation or redirected revenue streams. Our public services must rest on the foundation of sound finances. Labour will therefore set the target of eliminating the government's deficit on day-to-day spending within five years.

But government must have a laser-like focus on how we earn, as well as how we spend. At the same time as eliminating the current deficit, Labour will invest in our future, to ensure faster growth and help us to earn our way as a country again.

To maintain good fiscal health, we will have a firm rule in place to guide all our taxation and spending decisions. Our Fiscal Credibility Rule is based on the simple principle that government should not be borrowing for day-to-day spending, but that future growth depends on investment. It was designed in conjunction with world-leading economists. It also means we are committed to ensuring that the national debt is lower at the end of the next Parliament than it is today.

Compliance with the rule will be overseen by a strengthened and truly independent Office for Budget Responsibility, which we will make accountable to Parliament. We will also consult on implementing the recommendations of the Kerslake Review of the Treasury.

INFRASTRUCTURE INVESTMENT

Our country and its people have been held back by a lack of investment in the backbone of a modern economy – the infrastructure of transport, communications and energy systems. And when investment has happened, it has been too concentrated in too few places.

Labour will make different choices. We will take advantage of near-record low interest rates to create a National Transformation Fund that will invest £250 billion over ten years in upgrading our economy. We will ensure that the huge potential of every part of our country is met. The next Labour government will rebuild communities ripped apart by globalisation and neglected for years by government. We will rebuild and transform our economy so that it works for the many, not the few. So we will put in place tight rules to ensure that investment is fairly shared around every region and nation of the UK. We will tear down the barriers that have held too many people back.

A Labour government will complete the HS2 high-speed rail line from London through Birmingham to Leeds and Manchester, and then into Scotland, consulting with (and, where necessary, compensating) communities. We will link HS2 with other rail investments, such as Crossrail of the North (tying together our great northern cities) and on to the Durham Freight Centre. We will build a new Brighton Main Line for the South East.

In London, to ensure our capital continues to prosper, we will build Crossrail 2.

To harness the economic potential of new technologies and science, we will complete the Science Vale transport arc, from Oxford to Cambridge through Milton Keynes.

And we will deliver rail electrification and expansion across the whole country, including Wales and the South West.

We will transform our energy systems, investing in new, state-of-the-art low-carbon gas and renewable electricity production.

We will deliver universal superfast broadband availability by 2022. Labour will improve mobile internet coverage and expand provision of free public wi-fi in city centres and on public transport. We will improve 4G coverage and invest to ensure all urban areas, as well as major roads and railways, have uninterrupted 5G coverage. On day one we will instruct the National Infrastructure Commission to report on how to roll out 'ultrafast' (300Mbps) across the UK within the next decade.

UPGRADING OUR ECONOMY: LABOUR'S INDUSTRIAL STRATEGY

Our economy is suffering from years of neglect by governments that have refused to support our industries, businesses and workers. This wasted potential is holding us all back. Inequality has ballooned as the economy has shifted towards low-paid, insecure jobs.

Britain's manufacturing base has declined and we have relied too heavily on the financial sector, centred on London and the South East. And while the South East struggles with a rising cost of living crisis, many northern and coastal towns have watched as their economies and communities are left behind. Britain's failure to get all its regional and local economies working can be seen in the deterioration of the country's current account, weak productivity growth and underinvestment in infrastructure.

Britain can only be stronger if every nation and region is given the resources and support to succeed. Only a Labour government with a credible industrial strategy can reach this untapped potential and deliver prosperity to every corner of our country, working with devolved administrations.

Our industrial strategy will be built on objective, measurable missions designed to address the great challenges of our times. In meeting these challenges, we will move beyond the narrow approaches of the past, and mobilise the talents and resources of our whole country to deliver an economy fit for the future.

The first missions set by a Labour government will be to:

1. ensure that 60 per cent of the UK's energy comes from zero-carbon or renewable sources by 2030

2. create an innovation nation with the highest proportion of high-skilled jobs in the Organisation for Economic Co-operation and Development by 2030. We will meet the OECD target of 3 per cent of GDP spent on research and development by 2030.

In order to create a fertile ground for businesses to achieve these missions Labour will take action across the areas we know are necessary for business and industry to grow:

- Skills – by creating a National Education Service for England.

- Infrastructure – by investing £250 billion over the next ten years.

- UK supply chains – by targeting government support where there are gaps.

- Trade – by negotiating a new deal with Europe that puts jobs and the economy first.

- Procurement – by requiring the best standards on government contracts.

- Research and development – by committing extra research investment.

- Energy costs and security – by capping costs and investing in new publicly owned energy provision.

While our industrial strategy is one for growth across all sectors, Labour recognises that certain sectors are of strategic significance to the UK economy. For each strategic industry, the next Labour government will establish a council (modelled on the highly successful Automotive Council) to oversee its future security and growth. We will also encourage private investment by removing new plant and machinery from business rate calculations.

National and local government spends £200 billion a year in the private-sector procurement. Labour will put that spending power to good use to upgrade our economy, create good local jobs and reduce inequality. We will require firms supplying national or local government to meet the high standards we should expect of all businesses: paying their taxes, recognising trade unions, respecting workers' rights and equal opportunities, protecting the environment, providing training, and paying suppliers on time. We will expect

suppliers to reduce boardroom pay excesses by moving towards a 20:1 gap between the highest and lowest paid.

We will appoint a Digital Ambassador to liaise with technology companies to promote Britain as an attractive place for investment and provide support for start-ups to scale up to become world-class digital businesses. Our Digital Ambassador will help to ensure businesses are ready to grow and prosper in the digital age.

TRANSFORMING OUR FINANCIAL SYSTEM

A decade after the devastating international financial crisis, our financial system is still holding back too many of our small businesses and local economies.

Labour will transform how our financial system operates. Following the successful example of Germany and the Nordic countries, we will establish a National Investment Bank that will bring in private capital finance to deliver £250 billion of lending power.

This new public institution will support a network of regional development banks that, unlike giant City of London firms, will be dedicated to supporting inclusive growth in their communities. The banks will deliver the finance that our small businesses, co-operatives and innovative projects need across the whole country. The National Investment Bank will fill existing gaps in lending by private banks, particularly to small businesses, and by providing patient, long-term finance to R&D-intensive investments. It will also be given the task of helping to deliver our industrial strategy, by prioritising spending in line with its objectives.

Labour will overhaul the regulation of our financial system, putting in place a firm ring-fence between investment and retail banking that will protect consumers. We will take a new approach to the publicly-owned RBS, and launch a consultation on breaking up the bank to create new local public banks that are better matched to their customers' needs. And we will extend existing Stamp Duty Reserve Tax to cover a wider range of assets, ensuring that the public gets a fairer share of financial system profits.

Labour will change the law so that banks can't close a branch where there is a clear local need, putting their customers first. Britain has a successful international finance industry, but we also need a strong, safe and socially useful banking system to meet the needs of our own regional economies and communities. We will commit to creating a more diverse banking system, backed up by legislation.

A NEW DEAL FOR BUSINESS

The majority of businesses play by the rules: they pay their taxes and their workers reasonably and on time, and they operate with respect for the environment and local communities. That is why it is vital that government ensures that businesses doing the right thing are rewarded rather than undercut or outbid by those unscrupulous few that cut corners, whether on taxes, workers' conditions, environmental standards, or consumer safety and protection.

But our business culture doesn't always work like this. Scandals such as the failure of BHS show how the long-term growth of a company can be sacrificed for the sake of a quick buck.

When shareholders are looking for quick short-term returns, they encourage companies to cut corners. That means they look to cut wages, instead of investing for the long term, or they spend longer inventing new tax avoidance schemes than they do inventing new products.

By reforming the rules our companies operate under, we can make sure they stay focused on delivering shared wealth. Labour will amend company law so that directors owe a

duty directly not only shareholders, but to employees, customers, the environment and the wider public, and we will consult on bringing forward appropriate legislation within this Parliament.

Labour will amend the takeover regime to ensure that businesses identified as being 'systemically important' have a clear plan in place to protect workers and pensioners when a company is taken over. Labour will also legislate to reduce pay inequality by introducing an Excessive Pay Levy on companies with staff on very high pay.

Our small and medium-sized enterprises (SMEs) are the backbone of our economy, providing 60 per cent of private-sector jobs. Technological changes, like the spread of digital manufacturing and rapid communication, mean smaller, faster businesses will be the future of our economy.

Yet this Conservative Government has taken small businesses for granted. Labour is the party of small businesses. We understand the challenges our smaller businesses face. In order to provide the support many small businesses need, a Labour government will:

- Mandate the new National Investment Bank, and regional development banks in every region, to identify where other lenders fail to meet the needs of SMEs and prioritise lending to improve the funding gap.

- Reinstate the lower small-business corporation tax rate.

- Introduce a package of reforms to business rates – including switching from RPI to CPI indexation, exempting new investment in plant and machinery from valuations, and ensuring that businesses have access to a proper appeals process – while reviewing the entire business rates system in the longer run.

- Scrap quarterly reporting for businesses with a turnover of under £85,000.

- Declare war on late payments by:

  - Using government procurement to ensure that anyone bidding for a government contract pays its own suppliers within 30 days.

  - Developing a version of the Australian system of binding arbitration and fines for persistent late-payers for the private and public sectors.

We will also bring forward legislation to create a proper legal definition for co-operative ownership. The National Investment Bank and regional development banks will be charged with helping support our co-operative sector. Labour will aim to double the size of the co-operative sector in the UK, putting it on a par with those in leading economies like Germany or the US.

WIDENING OWNERSHIP OF OUR ECONOMY

Britain is a long-established democracy. But the distribution of ownership of the country's economy means that decisions about our economy are often made by a narrow elite. More democratic ownership structures would help our economy deliver for the many and lead to a fairer distribution of wealth.

In government, Labour would give more people a stake – and a say – in our economy by doubling the size of the co-operative sector and introducing a "right to own," making employees the buyer of first refusal when the company they work for is up for sale. We will act to 'insource' our public and local council services as preferred providers.

Many basic goods and services have been taken out of democratic control through privatisation. This has often led to higher prices and poorer quality, as prices are raised to pay out dividends. For example, water bills have increased 40 per cent since privatisation, and our private energy providers overcharged customers by £2 billion in 2015. In private hands, Royal Mail has increased stamp and parcel charges, and failed to meet its customer service obligations, while its owners trade shares at significant profit. The Conservative Government's privatisation of Royal Mail was a historic mistake, selling off another national asset on the cheap.

Across the world, countries are taking public utilities back into public ownership. Labour will learn from these experiences and bring key utilities back into public ownership to deliver lower prices, more accountability and a more sustainable economy. We will:

- Bring private rail companies back into public ownership as their franchises expire.

- Regain control of energy supply networks through the alteration of operator license conditions, and transition to a publicly owned, decentralised energy system.

- Replace our dysfunctional water system with a network of regional publicly-owned water companies.

- Reverse the privatisation of Royal Mail at the earliest opportunity.

Public ownership will benefit consumers, ensuring that their interests are put first and that there is democratic accountability for the service.

SUSTAINABLE ENERGY

Labour's energy policy is built on three simple principles:

- To ensure security of energy supply and 'keep the lights on'.

- To ensure energy costs are affordable for consumers and businesses.

- To ensure we meet our climate change targets and transition to a low-carbon economy.

The UK energy system is outdated, expensive and polluting. Privatisation has failed to deliver an energy system that delivers for people, businesses or our environment.

One in ten households are in fuel poverty, yet the Competition Markets Authority found customers are overcharged an enormous £2 billion every year.

Labour understands that many people don't have time to shop around, they just want reliable and affordable energy. So the next Labour Government will:

- Introduce an immediate emergency price cap to ensure that the average dual-fuel household energy bill remains below £1,000 per year, while we transition to a fairer system for bill payers.

- Take energy back into public ownership to deliver renewable energy, affordability for consumers, and democratic control. We will do this in the following stages:

  - Regaining control of energy supply networks through the alteration of the National and Regional Network Operator license conditions.

  - Supporting the creation of publicly owned, locally accountable energy companies and co-operatives to rival existing private energy suppliers, with at least one if every region.

  - Legislating to permit publicly owned local companies to purchase the regional grid infrastructure, and to ensure that national and regional grid infrastructure is brought into public ownership over time.

Labour will insulate four million homes as an infrastructure priority to help those who suffer in cold homes each winter. This will cut emissions, improve health, save on bills, and reduce fuel poverty and winter deaths.

Homeowners will be offered interest-free loans to improve their property. For renters, Labour will improve on existing Landlord Energy Efficiency regulations and re-establish the Landlord Energy Saving Allowance to encourage the uptake of efficiency measures.

Labour will ban fracking because it would lock us into an energy infrastructure based on fossil fuels, long after the point in 2030 when the Committee on Climate Change says gas in the UK must sharply decline.

Emerging technologies such as carbon capture and storage will help to smooth the transition to cleaner fuels and to protect existing jobs as part of the future energy mix. To safeguard the offshore oil and gas industry, we will provide a strategy focused on protecting vital North Sea assets, and the jobs and skills that depend on them.

We are committed to renewable energy projects, including tidal lagoons, which can help create manufacturing and energy jobs as well as contributing to climate-change commitments.

The UK has the world's oldest nuclear industry, and nuclear will continue to be part of the UK energy supply. We will support further nuclear projects and protect nuclear workers' jobs and pensions. There are considerable opportunities for nuclear power and decommissioning both internationally and domestically.

Building a clean economy of the future is the most important thing we must do for our children, our grandchildren and future generations. Yet recent years have seen a failure to progress towards our targets. A Labour government will put us back on track to meet the targets in the Climate Change Act and the Paris Agreement.

The low-carbon economy is one of the UK's fastest-growing sectors, creating jobs and providing investment across each region. It employed an estimated 447,000 employees in the UK in 2015 and saw over £77 billion in turnover. With backing from a Labour government, these sectors can secure crucial shares of global export markets.

Currently, the UK buys and sells energy tariff free from Europe, an arrangement which saves families and businesses money, and helps balance the power grid. As part of the Brexit negotiations, Labour will prioritise maintaining access to the internal energy market. Labour will also retain access to Euratom, to allow continued trade of fissile material, with access and collaboration over research vital to our nuclear industry.

CHAPTER 02

NEGOTIATING BREXIT

NEGOTIATING BREXIT

Labour accepts the referendum result and a Labour government will put the national interest first. We will prioritise jobs and living standards, build a close new relationship with the EU, protect workers' rights and environmental standards, provide certainty to EU nationals and give a meaningful role to Parliament throughout negotiations.

We will end Theresa May's reckless approach to Brexit, and seek to unite the country around a Brexit deal that works for every community in Britain.

We will scrap the Conservatives' Brexit White Paper and replace it with fresh negotiating priorities that have a strong emphasis on retaining the benefits of the Single Market and the Customs Union – which are essential for maintaining industries, jobs and businesses in Britain. Labour will always put jobs and the economy first.

A Labour government will immediately guarantee existing rights for all EU nationals living in Britain and secure reciprocal rights for UK citizens who have chosen to make their lives in EU countries. EU nationals do not just contribute to our society: they are part of our society. And they should not be used as bargaining chips.

It is shameful that the Prime Minister rejected repeated attempts by Labour to resolve this issue before Article 50 was triggered. As a result three million EU nationals have suffered unnecessary uncertainty, as have the 1.2 million UK citizens living in the EU.

A Conservative Brexit will weaken workers' rights, deregulate the economy, slash corporate taxes, sideline Parliament and democratic accountability, and cut Britain off from our closest allies and most important trading partners.

Labour recognises that leaving the EU with 'no deal' is the worst possible deal for Britain and that it would do damage to our economy and trade. We will reject 'no deal' as a viable option and if needs be negotiate transitional arrangements to avoid a 'cliff-edge' for the UK economy.

The issues that affect our continent now will continue to do so in the future – and Labour will continue to work constructively with the EU and other European nations on issues such as climate change, refugee crises and counter-terrorism. We will build a close co-operative future relationship with the EU, not as members but as partners.

A Labour government will ensure that the UK maintains our leading research role by seeking to stay part of Horizon 2020 and its successor programmes and by welcoming research staff to the UK. We will seek to maintain membership of (or equivalent relationships with) European organisations which offer benefits to the UK such as Euratom and the European Medicines Agency. We will seek to ensure that Britain remains part of the Erasmus scheme so that British students have the same educational opportunities after we leave the EU.

The EU is the UK's single largest trading partner in agricultural produce, with the vast majority of British exports being sold to European markets. A Labour government will end the uncertainty for our farmers and food producers by securing continued EU market access allowing British farmers and food producers to continue to sell their products on the Continent.

Labour will also protect our farmers and rural economy by ensuring Britain continues to set the highest standards in food quality and welfare. We will not allow Brexit to be used as an excuse to undercut our farmers and flood Britain's food chain with cheap and inferior produce.

We will drop the Conservatives' Great Repeal Bill, replacing it with an EU Rights and Protections Bill that will ensure there is no detrimental change to workers' rights, equality law, consumer rights or environmental protections as a result of Brexit.

Throughout the Brexit process, we will make sure that all EU-derived laws that are of benefit – including workplace laws, consumer rights and environmental protections – are

fully protected without qualifications, limitations or sunset clauses. We will work with trade unions, businesses and stakeholders to ensure there is a consensus on this vital issue. A Labour approach to Brexit will ensure there can be no rolling back of key rights and protections and that the UK does not lag behind Europe in workplace protections and environmental standards in future.

The EU has had a huge impact in securing workplace protections and environmental safeguards. But we all know that for many Brexiteers in the Tory Party, this was why they wanted to Leave – to tear up regulations and weaken hard-fought rights and protections.

A Labour government will never consider these rights a burden or accept the weakening of workers' rights, consumer rights or environmental protections.

We will introduce legislation to ensure there are no gaps in national security and criminal justice arrangements as a result of Brexit.

Labour recognises the vital role that cross-border agencies such as Eurojust and Europol have played in making Britain safer and that European Arrest Warrants have been invaluable. A Labour government will seek to retain membership of these agencies and continue European Arrest Warrant arrangements.

Labour will seek a Brexit deal that delivers for all regions and nations of the UK. We will introduce a 'presumption of devolution' where devolved powers transferred from the EU will go straight to the relevant region or nation. For many people and for much of our country, power can feel just as remote and unaccountable in Westminster as it does in Brussels. So a Labour government will seek to put powers as close to communities as possible.

We will ensure there is no drop in EU Structural Funding as a result of Brexit until the end of the current EU funding round in 2019/20. As part of Labour's plans to rebalance and rebuild the economy, we will ensure that no region or nation of the UK is affected by the withdrawal of EU funding for the remainder of this Parliament. This will also apply to the funding of peace and reconciliation projects in Northern Ireland.

We will also improve engagement and dialogue with the devolved administrations and seek to ensure the final Brexit deal addresses specific concerns. In particular Labour will ensure there is no return to a hard border between Northern Ireland and the Republic of Ireland and that there is no change in the status or sovereignty of Gibraltar. We will also protect Gibraltar's economy and ensure that its

government can continue to create jobs and prosperity in the years to come.

Where Theresa May wants to shut down scrutiny and challenge, Labour will welcome it. We will work with Parliament, not against it. On an issue of this importance the Government can't hide from the public or Parliament.

A Labour approach to Brexit also means legislating to guarantee that Parliament has a truly meaningful vote on the final Brexit deal.

IMMIGRATION

Labour offers fair rules and reasonable management of migration. In trade negotiations our priorities favour growth, jobs and prosperity. We make no apologies for putting these aims before bogus immigration targets.

Freedom of movement will end when we leave the European Union. Britain's immigration system will change, but Labour will not scapegoat migrants nor blame them for economic failures.

Labour will develop and implement fair immigration rules. We will not discriminate between people of different races or creeds. We will end indefinite detentions and distinguish between migrant labour and family attachment and will continue to support the work of the Forced Marriage Unit. We will replace income thresholds with a prohibition on recourse to public funds. New rules will be equally informed by negotiations with the EU and other partners, including the Commonwealth.

Whatever our trade arrangements, we will need new migration management systems, transparent and fair to everybody. Working with businesses, trade unions, devolved governments and others to identify specific labour and skill shortages.

Working together we will institute a new system which is based on our economic needs, balancing controls and existing entitlements. This may include employer sponsorship, work permits, visa regulations or a tailored mix of all these which works for the many, not the few.

Labour will protect those already working here, whatever their ethnicity. Our National Education Service will raise the level of skills and training. We will take decisive actions to end the exploitation of migrant labour undercutting workers' pay and conditions.

Labour will crack down on unscrupulous employers. We will stop overseas-only recruitment practices, strengthen safety-at-work inspections and increase prosecutions of employers evading the minimum wage.

Working with trade unions, we will end workplace exploitation.

Labour values the economic and social contributions of immigrants. Both public and private sector employers depend on immigrants. We will not denigrate those workers. We value their contributions, including their tax contributions.

For areas where immigration has placed a strain on public services we will reinstate the Migrant Impact Fund and boost it with a contributory element from the investments required for High Net Worth Individual Visas. Labour will restore the rights of migrant domestic workers, and end this form of modern slavery.

Labour will ease the underlying pressures in any areas struggling to cope with seven years of austerity by our programme of investments. We will not cut public services and pretend the cuts are a consequence of immigration.

Refugees are not migrants. They have been forced from their homes, by war, famine or other disasters. Unlike the Tories, we will uphold the proud British tradition of honouring the spirit of international law and our moral obligations by taking our fair share of refugees. The current arrangements for housing and dispersing refugees are not fit for purpose. They are not fair to refugees or to our communities. We will review these arrangements.

Labour welcomes international students who benefit and strengthen our education sector, generating more than £25 billion for the British economy and significantly boosting regional jobs and local businesses. They are not permanent residents and we will not include them in immigration numbers, but we will crack down on fake colleges.

INTERNATIONAL TRADE

Labour is pro-trade and pro-investment. The UK's future prosperity depends on minimising tariff and non-tariff barriers that prevent us from exporting and creating the jobs and economic growth we need.

A Labour government will work with devolved administrations to bring forward an integrated trade and industrial strategy that boosts exports, investment and decent jobs in Britain.

Labour will set out our priorities in an International Trade White Paper to lead a national debate on the future of Britain's trade policy. We will ensure proper transparency and parliamentary scrutiny of all future trade and investment deals.

The EU accounts for 44 per cent of our current exports and will continue to be a priority trading partner. As our trading relationship with the EU changes it is vital that we retain unrestricted access for our goods and services.

Through our Just Trading initiative launched in 2016, Labour will work with global trading partners to develop 'best-in-class' free trade and investment agreements that remove trade barriers and promote skilled jobs and high standards. We will ensure all future trade deals safeguard the right to regulate in the public interest and to protect public services.

Labour is committed to the rules-based international trading system of the World Trade Organisation (WTO). We will rejoin the Government Procurement Agreement, whilst safeguarding the capacity for public bodies to make procurement decisions in keeping with public policy objectives.

Labour will build human rights and social justice into trade policy. We will ensure that trade agreements cannot undermine human rights and labour standards, and that UK Export Finance support is not available to companies engaged in bribery or corrupt practices.

We will work with other WTO members to end the dumping of state-subsidised goods on our markets. The Conservatives consistently blocked EU efforts to respond to such dumping with the duties needed to defend the British steel industry. Labour will develop the full range of trade remedies necessary to support key sectors affected by these unfair practices.

Labour will champion the export interests of SMEs, ensuring all new trade agreements include a commitment to support their market access needs. We will develop an

export incentive scheme for SMEs based on international best practice, and we will ring-fence Tradeshow Access Programme grants to help SMEs reach new customers around the world.

Labour will use the full range of export credit, finance, insurance and trade promotion tools to boost British exports and support priority industrial sectors.

We will create a network of regional trade and investment champions to promote the export and investment interests of businesses across the country, and we will include regional representation on overseas trade missions.

Labour is committed to growing the digital economy and ensuring that trade agreements do not impede cross-border data flows, whilst maintaining strong data protection rules to protect personal privacy.

As part of our commitment to a low-carbon future, we will actively support international negotiations towards an Environmental Goods Agreement at the WTO. Labour will use trade negotiations to boost market access for British environmental goods and services, alongside support for investment into new green technologies and innovative low-carbon products.

Labour will develop capital investment schemes and other incentives to encourage investment into the UK, especially into target areas identified by the industrial strategy. We will champion the UK as a safe investment environment.

Labour will review our historic investment treaties with other countries, ensuring they are fit for purpose for the 21st century. Labour opposes parallel investor-state dispute systems for multinational corporations and we will open a dialogue with trading partners on alternative options that provide investor protection whilst guaranteeing equality before the law.

CHAPTER 03

TOWARDS A NATIONAL EDUCATION SERVICE

TOWARDS A NATIONAL EDUCATION SERVICE

Education is what empowers us all to realise our full potential. When it fails, it isn't just the individual that is held back, but all of us. When we invest in people to develop their skills and capabilities, we all benefit from a stronger economy and society.

At a time when working lives and the skills our economy needs are changing rapidly, governments have the responsibility to make lifelong learning a reality by giving everyone the opportunity to access education throughout their lives.

To meet this responsibility, Labour will create a unified National Education Service (NES) for England to move towards cradle-to-grave learning that is free at the point of use. The NES will be built on the principle that 'Every Child – and Adult – Matters' and will incorporate all forms of education, from early years through to adult education.

When the 1945 Labour government established the NHS, it created one of the central institutions of fairness of the 20th century. The NES will do the same for the 21st, giving people confidence and hope by making education a right, not a privilege, and building bridges where the Conservatives build barriers.

EARLY YEARS

Currently, there is a gap between the end of maternity leave and the beginning of full-time schooling. This gap can make it difficult for parents, particularly women, to return to work, unless they have access to informal childcare support. There is also extensive evidence that early years education has a major impact on child development, and that time in a formal education setting for young children can improve performance at GCSE and beyond.

Labour would seek to roll out educational provision for early years children as part of a National Education Service that is truly cradle-to-grave.

Labour introduced free childcare hours for parents, which were fully funded and resourced.

Under the Conservatives, the free hours entitlement is chronically under-funded, with provision patchy and hard to navigate. Many providers now simply refuse to participate in the scheme. The result is that many parents aren't even getting the hours they're entitled to.

Labour would:

1. Overhaul the existing childcare system in which subsidies are given directly to parents who often struggle to use them, and transition to a system of high-quality childcare places in mixed environments with direct government subsidy.

2. Maintain current commitments on free hours and make significant capital investment during our first two years of government, to ensure that the places exist to meet demand.

3. Phase in subsidised provision on top of free-hour entitlements, to ensure that everyone has access to affordable childcare, no matter their working pattern.

4. Transition to a qualified, graduate-led workforce, by increasing staff wages and enhancing training opportunities. This will benefit staff, who are among our worst-paid workers, and improve child development.

5. Extend the 30 free hours to all two-year-olds, and move towards making some childcare available for one-year-olds and extending maternity pay to 12 months.

Sure Start, and the support it gives to vulnerable and hard-to-reach parents, was one of the great achievements of the previous Labour government, but under the Conservatives 1,200 Sure Start centres have been lost. Labour will halt the closures and increase the amount of money available for Sure Start.

SCHOOLS

Conservative cuts are starving schools of the funding they need to deliver a first class education. Crippling underfunding is driving up class sizes and forcing schools to cut corners. A narrow curriculum and a culture of assessment is driving away teachers, creating a recruitment and retention crisis.

Labour will not waste money on inefficient free schools and the Conservatives' grammar schools vanity project. Labour does not want a return to secondary moderns. We will also oppose any attempt to force schools to become academies.

Labour's schools policy will be built on the following four foundations:

1. Investment – we will make sure schools are properly resourced by reversing the Conservatives' cuts and ensuring that all schools have the resources they need. We will introduce a fairer funding formula that leaves no school worse off, while redressing the historical underfunding of certain schools. Labour will also invest in new school buildings, including the phased removal of asbestos from existing schools.

2. Quality – we will drive up standards across the board, learning from examples of best practice, such as Labour's London Challenge, to encourage co-operation and strong leadership across schools. We and trust in teachers and support staff professionalism to refocus their workload on what happens in the classroom.

3. Accountability – Labour will ensure that all schools are democratically accountable, including appropriate controls to see that they serve the public interest and their local communities. We will require joined-up admissions policies across local schools to enable councils to fulfil their responsibilities on child places,
to simplify the admissions process for parents and to ensure that no child slips through the net.

4. Inclusion – Every child is unique, and a Labour-led education system will enable each to find their learning path through a wide choice of courses and qualifications. We will invest in measures to close the attainment gap between children from different backgrounds.

To give all children the best start in life, we will reduce class sizes to less than 30 for all five-, six-, and seven-year-olds, and seek to extend that as resources allow.

To aid attainment, we will introduce free school meals for all primary school children, paid for by removing the VAT exemption on private school fees.

We will abandon plans to reintroduce baseline assessments and launch a commission to look into curriculum and assessment, starting by reviewing Key Stage 1 and 2 SATs. The world's most successful education systems use more continuous assessment, which avoids 'teaching for the test'.

We will tackle the teacher recruitment and retention crisis by ending the public-sector pay cap, giving teachers more direct involvement in the curriculum, and tackling rising workloads by reducing monitoring and bureaucracy.

We will also consult on introducing teacher sabbaticals and placements with industry to encourage interaction between education and industry and introduce broad experiences into the classroom.

We will reintroduce the Schools Support Staff Negotiating Body and national pay settlements for teachers.

We will put £150 million back into supporting our children in schools by scrapping the Conservatives' nonsensical plans for schools to pay the apprenticeship levy.

We will extend schools-based counselling to all schools to improve children's mental health, at a cost of £90 million per year.

And we will deliver a strategy for children with special educational needs and disabilities (SEND) based on inclusivity, and embed SEND more substantially into training for teachers and non-teaching staff, so that staff, children and their parents are properly supported.

SKILLS

At a time when technology is changing demand for different kinds of skills, and evolving patterns of work mean that people are more likely to pursue several careers during their working lives, it is crucial that our education system enables people to upskill and retrain over their lifetimes. As part of our dynamic industrial strategy, lifelong training will deliver productivity and growth to the whole economy while transforming the lives of individuals and communities.

To ensure that we deliver for every part of the UK, we will devolve responsibility for skills, wherever there is an appetite, to city regions or devolved administrations.

Further and Adult Education

Despite claiming to be committed to delivering high-quality training, the Conservatives have ruthlessly cut funding for FE colleges – our main provider of adult and vocational education – and reduced entitlements for adult learners. This has led to diminishing numbers of courses and students, and plunged the sector into crisis.

Labour would introduce free, lifelong education in Further Education (FE) colleges, enabling everyone to upskill or retrain at any point in life.

Our skills and training sector has been held back by repeated reorganisation, which deprives providers, learners and employers of the consistency they need to assess quality. Labour would abandon Conservative plans to once again reinvent the wheel by building new technical colleges, redirecting the money to increase teacher numbers in the FE sector.

We share the broad aims of the Sainsbury Review but would ensure vocational routes incorporate the service sector as well as traditional manufacturing, working in tandem with our broad industrial strategy to deliver for the whole economy.

We will improve careers advice and open up a range of routes through, and back into, education, striking a balance between classroom and on-the-job training, to ensure students gain both technical and soft skills.

To implement the Sainsbury recommendations, we would correct historic neglect of the FE sector by giving the sector the investment – in teachers and facilities – it deserves to become a world-leading provider of adult and vocational education.

More specifically, we would:

- Bring funding for 16 to18-year-olds in line with Key Stage 4 baselines, while ensuring that the budget is distributed fairly between colleges and school sixth forms

- Restore the Education Maintenance Allowance for 16 to 18-year-olds from lower and middle income backgrounds

- Replace Advanced Learner Loans and upfront course fees with direct funding, making FE courses free at the point of use, including English for Speakers of Other Languages (ESOL) courses.

- Drive up quality and consistency in the FE sector by:

  - Encouraging co-operation and leadership across colleges and sixth forms, improving curriculum breadth and quality

  - Setting a target, backed up by funding, for all FE teaching staff to have a teaching qualification within five years.

- In recognition of the role played by private-sector providers, we would extend support for training to teachers in the private sector

- Increase capital investment to equip colleges to deliver T-levels and an official pre-apprenticeship trainee programme.

Apprenticeships

Employer-led training is the most effective way of meeting our growing skills gap. Labour supports the apprenticeship levy, but will take steps to ensure that every apprenticeship is of a high quality.

Labour will:

- Maintain the apprenticeship levy while taking measures to ensure high quality by requiring the Institute for Apprenticeships and Technical Education to report on an annual basis to the Secretary of State on quality outcomes of completed apprenticeships to ensure they deliver skilled workers for employers and real jobs for apprentices at the end of their training. And we will work with the devolved administrations to improve the operation of the levy

- Set a target to double the number of completed apprenticeships at NVQ level 3 by 2022

- Give employers more flexibility in how the levy is deployed, including allowing the levy to be used for pre-apprenticeship programmes

- Guarantee trade union representation in the governance structures of the Institute of Apprenticeships

- Protect the £440 million funding for apprenticeships for small-and medium-sized employers who don't pay the levy

- Set targets to increase apprenticeships for people with disabilities, care leavers and veterans, and ensure broad representation of women, BAME, LGBT and people with disabilities in all kinds of apprenticeships

- Consult on introducing incentives for large employers to over-train numbers of apprentices to fill skills gaps in the supply chain and the wider sector

- Reverse cuts to Unionlearn

- Set up a commission on Lifelong Learning tasked with integrating further and higher education.

HIGHER
EDUCATION

Labour believes education should be free, and we will restore this principle. No one should be put off educating themselves for lack of money or through fear of debt.

There is a real fear that students are being priced out of university education. Last year saw the steepest fall in university applications for 30 years.

Since the Conservatives came to power, university tuition fees have been trebled to over £9,000 a year, and maintenance grants have been abolished and replaced with loans.

The average student now graduates from university, and starts their working life, with debts of £44,000.

Labour will reintroduce maintenance grants for university students, and we will abolish university tuition fees.

University tuition is free in many northern European countries, and under a Labour government it will be free here too.

CHAPTER 04

A FAIR DEAL AT WORK

A FAIR DEAL AT WORK

Work should provide people with security and fulfilment. But for too many people work is insecure and does not make ends meet.

The Conservatives boast about the recovery of employment, but our labour market is failing. Real-terms pay is still lower than before the crash, and jobs are increasingly low skilled and insecure.

A Labour government will invest in enforcement through a new Ministry of Labour, and empower workers and their trade unions – because we are stronger when we stand together.

So we will review the rules on union recognition so that more workers have the security of a union.

At the same time as strengthening workers' rights, we will make work more fulfilling by using public investment to upgrade our economy and create high-quality jobs. While the Conservatives stand back and allow insecure work to spread, Labour will act to guarantee good jobs and businesses.

RIGHTS AT WORK

The next Labour government will bring in a 20-point plan for security and equality at work:

1. Give all workers equal rights from day one, whether part-time or full-time, temporary or permanent – so that working conditions are not driven down.

2. Ban zero hours contracts – so that every worker gets a guaranteed number of hours each week.

3. Legislate to ensure that any employer wishing to recruit labour from abroad does not undercut workers at home – because it causes divisions when one workforce is used against another.

4. Repeal the Trade Union Act and roll out sectoral collective bargaining – because the most effective way to maintain good rights at work is collectively through a union.

5. Guarantee trade unions a right to access workplaces – so that unions can speak to members and potential members.

6. Propose four new public holidays – bringing our country together to mark our four national patron saints' days. These will be additional to statutory holiday entitlement so that workers in Britain get the same proper breaks as in other countries.

7. Raise the Minimum Wage to the level of the Living Wage (expected to be at least £10 per hour by 2020) – for all workers aged 18 or over, so that work pays.

8. End the Public Sector Pay Cap – because public sector workers deserve a pay rise after years of falling wages.

9. Amend the takeover code to ensure every takeover proposal has a clear plan in place to protect workers and pensioners – because workers shouldn't suffer when a company is sold.

10. Roll out maximum pay ratios of 20:1 in the public sector and in companies bidding for public contracts – because it cannot be right that wages at the top keep rising while everyone else's stagnates.

11. Ban unpaid internships – because it's not fair for some to get a leg up when others can't afford to.

12. Enforce all workers' rights to trade union representation at work – so that all workers can be supported when negotiating with their employer.

13. Abolish employment tribunal fees – so that people have access to justice.

14. Double paid paternity leave to four weeks and increase paternity pay – because fathers are parents too and deserve to spend more time with their new babies.

15. Strengthen protections for women against unfair redundancy – because no one should be penalised for having children.

16. Hold a public inquiry into blacklisting – to ensure that blacklisting truly becomes and remains a thing of the past.

17. Give equalities reps statutory rights – so they have time to protect workers from discrimination.

18. Reinstate protection against third party harassment – because everyone deserves to be safe at work.

19. Use public spending power to drive up standards, including only awarding public contracts to companies which recognise trade unions.

20. Introduce a civil enforcement system to ensure compliance with gender pay auditing – so that all workers have fair access to employment and promotion opportunities and are treated fairly at work.

A Labour government will ensure Britain abides by the global Labour standards of the ILO conventions.

All workers should be able to work in a safe environment and return to their families at the end of the day. Labour will enforce regulations that save lives.

As well as legislating against zero hours contracts, there are many more workers on short hours contracts (some only guaranteed a few hours per week), but who regularly work far more. We will strengthen the law so that those who work regular hours for more than 12 weeks will have a right to a regular contract, reflecting those hours.

We will also scrap the changes brought in by the Conservatives in 2014 to TUPE, which weakened the protections for workers transferring between contractors, and we will abolish the loophole to the agency workers regulations known as the Swedish derogation.

We will consult with employers and trade unions on legislating for statutory bereavement leave, for time off work after the loss of close family members. We will also consult on toughening the law against assaulting workers who have to enforce laws such as age-related sales or ticketing arrangements, and who face regular abuse.

Labour will maintain the ACAS Early Conciliation System to try to solve workplace issues efficiently, and we will protect the current compromise on Sunday trading hours.

Labour will also legislate to permit secure online and workplace balloting for industrial action votes and internal union elections.

Workers in Britain are among the easiest and cheapest to make redundant, meaning when multinational companies are taking decisions to downsize that British workers are at a disadvantage. We will consult with trade unions and industry on reviewing redundancy arrangements to bring workers in Britain more into line with their European counterparts.

Stagnating incomes have forced many to take on more debt. Labour will introduce a version of Scotland's Debt Arrangement Scheme to give breathing space to households struggling with high debts.

SELF-EMPLOYED WORKERS

Self-employment can bring many benefits, freedoms and flexibilities to people – and is a vital and often entrepreneurial sector of our economy.

But there is also mounting evidence that workers are being forced into self-employment by unscrupulous employers to avoid costs and their duties to workers. Labour will clamp down on bogus self-employment by:

- Shifting the burden of proof, so that the law assumes a worker is an employee unless the employer can prove otherwise.

- Imposing punitive fines on employers not meeting their responsibilities, helping to deter others from doing the same.

- Involving trade unions in enforcement, e.g. by giving them a seat on the executive board of the new Ministry of Labour.

- Giving the Ministry of Labour the resources to enforce all workers' rights.

- Banning payroll companies, sometimes known as umbrella companies, which create a false structure to limit employers' tax liabilities and limit workers' rights.

- Giving employment agencies and end-users joint responsibility for ensuring that the rights of agency workers are enforced.

- Rolling out sectoral collective bargaining and strengthening trade union rights, because empowering people to claim their own rights in the workplace is the most effective means of enforcement.

We would also extend the rights of employees to all workers, including shared parental pay, making a substantial and immediate difference to the quality of life of people in insecure work. But there are real concerns that rapid changes to the world of work are rendering existing employment categories outdated.

Labour recognises that the law often struggles to keep up with the ever-changing new forms of employment and work, so we will set up a dedicated commission to modernise the law around employment status. New statutory definitions of employment status would reduce the need for litigation and improve compliance.

The commission will be led by legal and academic experts with representation from industry and trade unions.

CHAPTER 05

SOCIAL SECURITY

SOCIAL SECURITY

After seven years of rising poverty and inequality, Labour will rebuild and transform our social security system. Like the NHS, our social security system is there for all of us in our time of need, providing security and dignity in retirement and the basics in life should we become sick or disabled, or fall on hard times.

DIGNITY FOR PENSIONERS

Labour will always be on the side of pensioners and help ensure security and dignity for older people in retirement.

As the Conservatives abandon their commitments to older people, Labour will guarantee the state pension 'triple lock' throughout the next Parliament. It will rise by at least 2.5 per cent a year or be increased to keep pace with inflation or earnings, whichever is higher.

The Winter Fuel Allowance and free bus passes will also be guaranteed as universal benefits.

We will protect the pensions of UK citizens living overseas in the EU or further afield.

Over 2.5 million women born in the 1950s have had their state pension age changed without fair notification. These women deserve both recognition for the injustice they have suffered and some kind of compensation for their losses.

Alongside our commitment to extend Pension Credit to hundreds of thousands of the most vulnerable women, Labour is exploring options for further transitional protections, to ensure that all these women have security and dignity in older age.

This must never happen again. Labour will legislate so that accrued rights to the basic state pension cannot be changed, but future benefits can.

The pension age is due to rise to 66 by the end of 2020. Labour rejects the Conservatives' proposal to increase the state pension age even further. We will commission a new review of the pension age, specifically tasked with developing a flexible retirement policy to reflect both the contributions made by people, the wide variations in life expectancy, and the arduous conditions of some work.

We'll restore confidence in the workplace pension system and put people rather than profit at its centre. Labour will end rip-off

hidden fees and charges, and enable the development of large efficient pensions funds, which will mean more cash for scheme members and lower costs for employers.

A Labour government will commit to an immediate review of the mineworkers' pension scheme and British Coal superannuation scheme surplus, sharing arrangements between government and scheme beneficiaries.

DIGNITY FOR THOSE WHO CANNOT WORK

Poverty in Britain is rising due to the Conservatives' attempts to balance the books on the backs of the poorest. They have slashed social security over the last seven years, leaving more people in poverty, subject to a punitive sanctions regime, and reliant on food banks.

Labour will act immediately to end the worst excesses of the Conservative government's changes. We will:

- Scrap the punitive sanctions regime

- Scrap the Bedroom Tax

- Reinstate Housing Benefit for under-21s

- Scrap cuts to Bereavement Support Payment.

The cuts to work allowances in Universal Credit (UC), and the decision to limit tax credit and UC payments to the first two children in a family, are an attack on low-income families and will increase child poverty. Labour will reform and redesign UC, ending six-week delays in payment and the 'rape clause'.

With nearly four million children currently living in poverty, the majority in working families, we will commit to tackle child poverty with a new Child Poverty Strategy.

The Tories have completely failed on their promise of making work pay and on tackling the barriers to work faced by people with disabilities.

Labour supports a social model of disability. People may have a condition or an impairment but they are disabled by society. We need to remove the barriers in society that restrict opportunities and choices for people with disabilities.

We will build on the previous Labour government's commitment to people with disabilities in 2009 as signatories to the UN Convention on the Rights of Persons with Disabilities, and incorporate it into UK law.

Labour will repeal the following cuts in social security support to people with disabilities through a new Social Security Bill published in our first year in office. We will:

- Increase Employment and Support Allowance (ESA) by £30 per week for those in the work-related activity group, and repeal cuts in the UC limited capacity for work element.

- Increase Carer's Allowance by £11 to the level of Jobseekers' Allowance.

- Implement the court decision on Personal Independence Payment (PIP) so that there is real parity of

esteem between those with physical and mental-health conditions.

• Scrap the Work Capability and Personal Independence Payment assessments and replace them with a personalised, holistic assessment process that provides each individual with a tailored plan, building on their strengths and addressing barriers. Labour will end the privatisation of assessments.

• End the pointless stress of reassessments for people with severe long-term conditions.

• Commission a report into expanding the Access to Work programme.

We will change the culture of the social security system, from one that demonises people not in work to one that is supportive and enabling.

As well as scrapping the Conservatives' punitive sanctions regime, we will change how Jobcentre Plus staff are performance-managed.

Labour will strengthen access to justice for people with disabilities by enhancing the 2010 Equality Act, enabling discrimination at work to be challenged. We will ensure that under the Istanbul Convention, disability hate crime and violence against women with disabilities is reported annually, with national actions plans to address these issues.

CHAPTER 06

SECURE HOMES FOR ALL

SECURE HOMES FOR ALL

Home is at the heart of all of our lives. It's the foundation on which we raise our families, the bedrock for our dreams and aspirations. But for too many people, the housing pressures they face are getting worse not better. Britain has a housing crisis – a crisis of supply and a crisis of affordability.

After seven years of failure, the Conservatives have no plan to fix the housing crisis. Since 2010, housebuilding has fallen to its lowest level since the 1920s, rough sleeping has risen every year, rents have risen faster than incomes, there are almost 200,000 fewer home-owners, and new affordable housebuilding is at a 24-year low.

It doesn't have to be like this. Labour will invest to build over a million new homes. By the end of the next Parliament we will be building at least 100,000 council and housing association homes a year for genuinely affordable rent or sale.

Labour will establish a new Department for Housing to focus on tackling the crisis and to ensure housing is about homes for the many, not investment opportunities for the few. Labour's new housing ministry will be tasked with improving the number, standards and affordability of homes. We will overhaul the Homes and Communities Agency to be Labour's housing delivery body, and give councils new powers to build the homes local communities need.

We will prioritise brownfield sites and protect the green belt. We will start work on a new generation of New Towns to build the homes we need and avoid urban sprawl.

We will make the building of new homes, including council homes, a priority through our National Transformation Fund, as part of a joined-up industrial and skills strategy that ensures a vibrant construction sector with a skilled workforce and rights at work.

Labour will not only build more, we will build better. We will insulate more homes to help people manage the cost of energy bills, to reduce preventable winter deaths, and to meet our climate change targets. We will consult on new rules on minimum space standards to prevent 'rabbit hutch' properties and on new modern standards for building 'zero carbon homes'.

We will ensure that local plans address the need for older people's housing, ensuring that choice and downsizing options are readily available.

We will keep the Land Registry in public hands, where it belongs, and make ownership of land more transparent.

HOME
OWNERSHIP

The number of home-owning households has fallen by 900,000 for the under-45s since 2010.

Labour will back first-time buyers to buy that special first home. The number of affordable homes to buy has plummeted by two-thirds under the Conservatives, so we will build thousands more low-cost homes reserved for first-time buyers. We will guarantee Help to Buy funding until 2027 to give long-term certainty to both first-time buyers and the housebuilding industry. We will also give local people buying their first home 'first dibs' on new homes built in their area to give them confidence that new homes will be available to them and their families.

After seven years of failure under the Conservatives, Labour will build the new homes first-time buyers need – just as Labour councils have been doing right across the country, building an average of nearly 1,000 more new homes than Conservative councils.

We will back those who own their homes, including home-owners who own their home as leaseholders and who are currently unprotected from rises in 'ground rent' from developers or management companies. A Labour government will give leaseholders security from rip-off ground rents and end the routine use of leasehold houses in new developments.

PRIVATE RENTERS

We will end insecurity for private renters by introducing controls on rent rises, more secure tenancies, landlord licensing and new consumer rights for renters.

Soaring rents are a real problem – leading to more families living in temporary accommodation, more people sleeping rough, and many not having enough money to save up for a deposit or for a rainy day.

Labour will make new three-year tenancies the norm, with an inflation cap on rent rises. Given the particular pressures in London we will look at giving the Mayor the power to give renters in London additional security. We will legislate to ban letting agency fees for tenants.

We will also empower tenants to call time on bad landlords by giving renters new consumer rights. Renters are spending £9.6 billion a year on homes that the government classes as 'non-decent'. Around a quarter of this is paid by housing benefit. A Labour government would introduce new legal minimum standards to ensure properties are 'fit for human habitation' and empower tenants to take action if their rented homes are sub-standard.

We will reverse the cruel decision to abolish housing benefit for 18 to 21- year-olds, which risks putting even more vulnerable young people on our streets.

COUNCIL AND SOCIAL TENANTS

Under the Conservatives, affordable housebuilding has fallen to a 24-year low. Labour will build the genuinely affordable homes to rent and buy that the country needs.

We will remove government restrictions that stop councils building homes and begin the biggest council building programme for at least 30 years. We will ditch the Conservatives' ban on long-term council tenancies to give council tenants security in their homes. We want more people to have a secure tenancy in a home built to high standards.

Labour will scrap the punitive bedroom tax, which has caused many people to be evicted from their home and their community.

More council homes have been sold off under the Conservatives and only one in five have been replaced, despite long housing waiting lists. Labour will suspend the right-to-buy policy to protect affordable homes for local people, with councils only able to resume sales if they can prove they have a plan to replace homes sold like-for-like.

HOMELESSNESS

Homelessness is not inevitable in a country as decent and well off as ours. However, since 2010 the number of people sleeping rough in shop doorways and on park benches has more than doubled. This shames us all. There can be no excuses – it must end. Full stop.

More families are living in temporary accommodation, meaning 120,000 children spent last Christmas without a home to call their own.

This growing homelessness shames the Conservatives. The spiralling rise in street homelessness results directly from decisions made by the Conservatives on pay, housing, mental health and social security.

Labour will set out a new national plan to end rough sleeping within the next Parliament, starting by making available 4,000 additional homes reserved for people with a history of rough sleeping. We will also take action to tackle the root causes of homelessness, including safeguarding homeless hostels and other supported housing from crude Conservative cuts to housing benefit.

CHAPTER 07

HEALTHCARE FOR ALL

NHS

In the aftermath of war and national bankruptcy, it was a Labour government that found the resources to create a National Health Service – our proudest achievement, providing universal healthcare for all on the basis of need, free at the point of use.

Labour will invest in our NHS, to give patients the modern, well-resourced services they need for the 21st century. Labour will ensure that NHS patients get the world-class quality of care they need and that staff are able to deliver the standards that patients expect.

We will guarantee and uphold the standards of service to which patients are legally entitled under the NHS constitution. By guaranteeing access to treatment within 18 weeks, we will take one million people off NHS waiting lists by the end of the next Parliament. We will guarantee that patients can be seen in A&E within four hours. By properly resourcing the NHS, Labour will stop the routine breach of safe levels of bed occupancy, and we will end mixed-sex wards. We will deliver the Cancer Strategy for England in full by 2020, helping 2.5 million people living with cancer. And, by properly resourcing ambulance services, we will end the scandal of slowing ambulance-response times.

Labour will focus resources on services to provide care closer to home and deliver a truly 21st century health system. We will work towards a new model of community care that takes into account not only primary care but also social care and mental health. We will increase funding to GP services to ensure patients can access the care they need. And we will halt pharmacy cuts and review provision to ensure all patients have access to pharmacy services, particularly in deprived or remote communities.

Labour will tackle the growing problem of rationing of services and medicines across England, taking action to address 'postcode lotteries' and making sure that the quality of care you receive does not depend on which part of the country you live in. We will ensure all NHS patients get fast access to the most effective new drugs and treatments, and insist on value-for-money agreements with pharmaceutical companies.

To make sure that autistic people are able to access the whole of their community and to put an end to social isolation, Labour will set the ambition to make our country autism-friendly. We will ensure that everyone with a long-term condition, such as those with diabetes, will have the right to a specialised care plan, and access to condition-management education. We will ensure high-

quality, personalised care for people approaching the end of their life, wherever and whenever they need it.

Labour will ensure that NHS England completes the trial programme to provide PrEP (pre-exposure prophylaxis) as quickly as possible, and fully roll out the treatment to high-risk groups to help reduce HIV infection.

Labour will fund free parking in NHS England – for patients, staff and visitors – by increasing the tax on private medical insurance premiums.

Public health

For our health and care services to be sustainable in the long term, we need a renewed commitment to keeping people fit and well. Labour will focus our efforts on children's health, protecting the wellbeing of the nation for the decades to come.

We will take action to significantly reduce infant deaths and to ensure all families who lose a baby receive appropriate bereavement support.

Labour will invest in children's health, bringing in a new government ambition for our children to be the healthiest in the world. We will fight health inequalities to break the scandalous link between child ill-health and poverty. We will introduce a new Index of Child Health to measure progress against international standards, and report annually against four key indicators: obesity, dental health, under-fives and mental health. We will set up a new £250 million Children's Health Fund to support our ambitions. As part of a preventative healthcare drive, Labour will increase the number of health visitors and school nurses.

We will publish a new childhood obesity strategy within the first 100 days, with proposals on advertising and food labelling. We will make a concerted effort to address poor childhood oral health in England. Labour will implement the Soft Drinks Industry Levy, commonly known as the 'sugar tax'.

We will implement a strategy for the children of alcoholics based on recommendations drawn up by independent experts.

Labour will implement a Tobacco Control Plan, focusing on issues of mental health and young smokers.

Loneliness is an increasing problem for our society, and as Jo Cox put it, "young or old, loneliness doesn't discriminate". A Labour government will create a more equal society for the many by working with communities, civil society and business to reduce loneliness.

Labour will address historic public-health injustices. We will hold a public enquiry into contaminated blood. We will also hold a public inquiry into medicines, including Valproate, medical devices and medical products licensing and regulation.

A Labour government would maintain our commitment to improve sexual-health services, especially HIV services which will include reducing the rates of undiagnosed and late-diagnosed HIV, ending the stigma of HIV in society, and promoting the increased availability of testing and treatment.

NHS staff

To guarantee the best possible services for patients, Labour will invest in our health and care workforce. A Labour government will step in with a long-term workforce plan for our health service that gives staff the support they need to do the best for their patients.

Labour will scrap the NHS pay cap, put pay decisions back into the hands of the independent pay review body and give our NHS workers the pay they deserve. Labour will protect patients and legislate to ensure safe staffing levels in the NHS.

Labour's long-term ambition is for our health system to have the best trained staff in the world, ready to deal with whatever they have to face in the years to come. Labour will re-introduce bursaries and funding for health-related degrees. Labour will support doctors to deliver the best care possible by investing in the training, education and development of doctors throughout their careers.

Labour will immediately guarantee the rights of EU staff working in our health and care services. Labour will support NHS whistleblowers to make sure health service staff are able to speak up in support of the best possible standards for patients. Labour will make it an aggravated criminal offence to attack NHS staff.

NHS funding

Labour will commit to over £30 billion in extra funding over the next Parliament through increasing income tax for the highest 5 per cent of earners and by increasing tax on private medical insurance, and we will free up resources by halving the fees paid to management consultants.

Labour will boost capital funding for the NHS, to ensure that patients are cared for in buildings and using equipment that are fit for the 21st century. And we will introduce a new Office for Budget Responsibility for Health to oversee health spending and scrutinise how it is spent.

Labour will halt and review the NHS 'Sustainability and Transformation Plans', which are looking at closing health services across England, and ask local people to participate in the redrawing of plans with a focus on patient need rather than available finances. We will create a new quality, safety and excellence regulator – to be called 'NHS Excellence'.

The next Labour government will reverse privatisation of our NHS and return our health service into expert public control. Labour will repeal the Health and Social Care Act that puts profits before patients, and make the NHS the preferred provider. We will reinstate the powers of the Secretary of State for Health to have overall responsibility for the NHS.

We will introduce a new legal duty on the Secretary of State and on NHS England to ensure that excess private profits are not made out of the NHS at the expense of patient care.

TOWARDS A NATIONAL CARE SERVICE

Our social care sector is in crisis, with severe consequences for the quality of care, public finances, personal assets, pressures on unpaid carers of family and friends, and delays to discharging patients from hospitals.

Care services have been slowly but relentlessly privatised. In recent years, one in ten people reaching the age of 65 have faced lifetime care costs of over £100,000, with some homeowners paying the entire value of their homes.

The Conservatives' cuts have led to £4.6 billion lost from social care budgets, despite rising demand. Around 1.2 million older people have care needs that are going unmet. Care in the community has become a cover for unseen neglect.

In our first term, Labour will lay the foundations of a National Care Service for England.

Our first urgent task will be to address the immediate funding crisis. We will increase the social care budgets by a further £8 billion over the lifetime of the next Parliament, including an additional £1 billion for the first year. This will be enough for providers to pay a real living wage without cutting the quality of care they provide. It will allow implementation of the principles of the Ethical Care Charter, already adopted in 28 council areas, ending 15-minute care visits and providing care workers with paid travel time, access to training and an option to choose regular hours.

Labour will also increase the Carer's Allowance for unpaid full-time carers to align the benefit with rates of the Jobseeker's Allowance.

Short-term funding solutions will not address the fundamental long-term challenges of our ageing demographics, nor meet the growing demands arising from late-life illnesses.

The National Care Service will be built alongside the NHS, with a shared requirement for single commissioning, partnership arrangements, pooled budgets and joint working arrangements. We will build capacity to move quickly towards a joined-up service that will signpost users to all the appropriate services at the gateway through which they arrive.

In its first years, our service will require an additional £3 billion of public funds every year, enough to place a maximum limit on lifetime personal contributions to care costs, raise the asset threshold below which people are entitled to state support, and provide free end of life care. There are different ways the necessary monies can be raised. We will seek consensus on a cross-party basis about how it should be funded, with options including wealth taxes, an employer care contribution or a new social care levy.

Improving the quality of social care is a vital part of providing dignity in older age and independence and support for people who are vulnerable or have a disability or a mental health condition.

Labour will build a new National Care Service. We will also set out the funding alternatives clearly and honestly, seeking to implement change through consensus. Providing dignity and care in old age should transcend party politics and campaign slogans.

MENTAL HEALTH

Mental ill-health is the biggest unaddressed health challenge of our age. Around one in four people in the UK will experience a mental health problem each year.

Yet, since 2010 mental health funding has been cut, the number of mental health nurses has fallen by 6,600 and remaining mental health budgets have been raided to plug holes elsewhere in the NHS.

Labour will work to reverse the damage done to mental health services under this Tory government, which is particularly hitting services for LGBT and BAME communities.

In order to protect services, we will ring-fence mental health budgets and ensure funding reaches the frontline.

We will end the scandal of children being treated on adult mental health wards and stop people being sent across the country, away from their support networks, to secure the treatment they need by bringing forward the ending of out-of-area placements to 2019.

Labour will also bring an end to the neglect of children's mental health. Half of people with mental health problems as adults present with symptoms by the age of 14. Yet, across England only 8 per cent of mental health funding goes to services for children and young people. In recent years, referrals to Child and Adolescent Mental Health Services have increased by two-thirds, and the number of young people presenting to A&E units with psychiatric conditions has doubled. Suicide is now the most common cause of death for boys aged between five and 19.

Labour will invest in early intervention by increasing the proportion of mental health budgets spent on support for children and young people. We will ensure that access to a counselling service is available for all children in secondary schools.

Giving mental health the same priority as physical health means not only ensuring access to services, but also making improvements, to those services. Choice is important in a modern NHS, and patients who receive their therapy of choice have better outcomes. Labour will therefore ask the National Institute for Health and Care Excellence (NICE) to evaluate the potential for increasing the range of evidence-based psychological therapies on offer.

CHAPTER 08

SAFER COMMUNITIES

POLICE
AND CRIME

Last year, there were an estimated 6.1 million incidents of crime experienced by adults in England and Wales. Almost every police force in the country recorded an increase in crime, with worrying rises in some of the most violent offences, including gun and knife crime and homicide.

On Theresa May's watch, police numbers have been cut by 20,000. Cuts to the police force endanger communities and endanger police officers too. Labour's approach to policing crime will be different.

We will support the police in the performance of their duties. We will provide officers, police community support officers and civilian staff with the equipment and people they need to provide effective policing services, including from the growing threat of cybercrime. We will work with them to ensure that our communities are safer, for all of us.

We will champion community policing policies and incentivise good policing practice, working with Police and Crime Commissioners throughout the country on strategies to prevent crime. We will also work to eliminate institutional biases against BAME communities, that mean you are still far more likely to be stopped and searched as a black or Asian man.

Labour will recruit 10,000 more police officers to work on community beats, equivalent to at least one more for every neighbourhood in the country.

We will ensure appropriate support is provided to victims of crime and introduce legislation for minimum standard entitlements to service from criminal justice agencies.

The level of violence against women and girls is not acceptable. Labour will emphasise the safety of women and girls by appointing a commissioner to set new standards for tackling domestic and sexual violence. We will establish a National Refuge Fund and ensure stability for rape crisis centres. We will make age-appropriate sex and relationship education a compulsory part of the curriculum so young people can learn about respectful relationships. We will strengthen the law, banning the use of community resolutions as a response to domestic violence.

Labour will continue to enforce effective measures to prevent all forms of abuse, including female genital mutilation.

Security and counter-terrorism

Labour will maintain the cross-border security co-operation agreements with our intelligence partners in Europe and beyond. We will always provide our security agencies with the resources and the powers they need to protect our country and keep us all safe. We will also ensure that such powers do not weaken our individual rights or civil liberties.

When – as they sometimes will – these aims collide, the exercise of investigatory powers must always be both proportionate and necessary. We will reintroduce effective judicial oversight over how and when they are used, when the circumstances demand that our collective security outweighs an individual freedom.

Labour will review the Prevent programme with a view to assessing both its effectiveness and its potential to alienate minority communities. In doing so, we will address the government's failure to take any effective new measures against a growing problem of extreme or violent radicalisation.

BORDER SECURITY

Border security is vital in preventing serious crimes including child abduction, people trafficking, smuggling of drugs and guns, terrorism and modern day slavery.

Contrary to the Conservative government's rhetoric, they have not taken control of our borders or strengthened our national security. Instead, they have suppressed the independent inspector's reports highlighting weaknesses in our borders and cut the Border Force by thousands of personnel. They want to turn private sector landlords, teachers, medical staff and other public sector workers into unpaid immigration officers, forcing them to provide information to the authorities.

The Conservatives promised and failed to deliver 100 per cent exit checks at the borders. Labour will recruit 500 more border guards to add to our safeguards and controls.

FIRE AND
RESCUE SERVICES

Labour will halt cuts to the Fire Service. The Conservatives have cut 10,000 firefighter jobs and closed dozens of fire stations. As a result, response times have got slower and lives have been put at risk.

Labour will recruit 3,000 new firefighters, review staffing levels, and consult on national minimum standards for the service. We will reinstate separate governance arrangements for Fire and Police Services.

We will give the Fire and Rescue Services a statutory duty to co-ordinate and respond to floods.

JUSTICE

We all need access to the justice system to protect us from those who would deny us our rights. Labour will set out to make Britain a fair society with liberties for all, governed by the rule of law, and in which the law is enforced equally.

The Conservatives threaten our Human Rights Act and may withdraw us from the European Convention of Human Rights. Labour will retain the Human Rights Act.

Justice is all too often denied. Too many ordinary people know this. There are football fans, trade unionists, environmental activists and people living with disabilities whose personal experiences provide first-hand testimony.

Labour will hold public inquiries into historic injustices. We will open inquiries into Orgreave and blacklisting. We will release all papers relating to the Shrewsbury 24 trials and the 37 Cammell Laird shipyard workers.

Justice today has become the preserve of the rich. Budget cuts mean that thousands are deprived of fair resolutions. Justice is eroded by the poor decisions of privatised assessments, by the withdrawal of legal aid, by the removal of appeal rights, by the delays arising from overcrowded courts and by the costs of fees.

Eligibility for legal aid has been withdrawn across a whole range of areas. This has had disturbing consequences for the delivery of justice.

Democracy is founded upon the rule of law and judicial independence. We will also review the judicial appointments process, to ensure a judiciary that is more representative of our society.

Labour will immediately re-establish early advice entitlements in the Family Courts. The shameful consequences of withdrawal have included a requirement for victims of domestic abuse to pay doctors for certification of their injuries. Labour's plans will remove that requirement. At the same time, we will legislate to prohibit the cross examination of victims of domestic violence by their abuser in certain circumstances.

We will reintroduce funding for the preparation of judicial review cases. Judicial review is an important way of holding government to account. There are sufficient safeguards to discourage unmeritorious cases.

We will review the legal aid means tests, including the capital test for those on income-related benefits.

Labour will consider the reinstatement of other legal aid entitlements after receiving the final recommendations of the Access to Justice Commission led by Lord Bach.

The justice system can be bewildering and intimidating. There are many improvements that can be made both to the law and to the court processes.

Labour will introduce a no-fault divorce procedure.

A Labour government will consult on establishing an environmental tribunal with simplified procedures to hear challenges to unlawful government decisions, like those made on the air quality strategy, without engaging in prohibitively expensive processes.

Labour will not prohibit the courts from raising monies to provide services, but we will introduce a ratio to establish the maximum difference between actual costs and charges levied.

Labour will continue to extend the use of technology in our court service where it enhances access to justice, timely dispute resolution and efficient administration.

PRISONS AND PROBATION SERVICE

Labour is tough on crime and tough on the causes of crime, but we won't make the lives of workers in the criminal justice system tougher. Prison officers, probation officers and other workers need the resources to do their jobs safely, effectively and successfully.

Our prisons are overcrowded. Staffing levels are too low. The situation is dangerous and violence against prison officers is rising. Riots and disturbances in our prisons are increasing. Prison escapes cause distress to people living near prisons.

A Labour government will publish annual reports on prisoner-staff ratios, with a view to maintaining safety and ending overcrowding.

We will recruit 3,000 more prison officers and review the training and professional development available. We will publish prison officer to prisoner ratios for all prisons. Our proposal to lift the public sector pay cap will help to increase the recruitment and retention of both prison officers and probation officers.

Re-offending rates are too high. The Conservatives talked of a rehabilitation revolution, and then just gave up. Their proposal now is to lock up more and more individuals, ignoring the evidence that our prisons are too often dumping grounds for people who need treatment more than they need punishment. Labour will insist on personal rehabilitation plans for all prisoners.

Prison should always be a last resort – the state's most severe sanction for serious offences. It should never be a substitute for failing mental health services, or the withdrawal of funding from drug treatment centres. We will review the provision of mental health services in prisons.

Under a Labour government, there will be no new private prisons and no public sector prisons will be privatised.

Labour's innovative models of youth justice successfully turned round the lives of many young people, steering them away from crime and towards more constructive ways. In government, we will again continue to innovate and incentivise local authorities, police forces and probation services to engage effectively with young people at risk of drifting into anti-social or criminal behaviours. We will embed restorative justice practices across all youth offending institutions.

The part-privatisation of probation services has already failed.

Labour will review the role of Community Rehabilitation Companies.

The Conservatives bulldozed changes to the probation service through despite warnings that they had not been tested and were founded on a weak evidence base.

CHAPTER 09

LEADING RICHER LIVES

LOCAL COMMUNITIES

Councils deliver vital local services to our communities, but their budgets have been slashed by Conservative cuts. This has led to a deterioration of local services, from bin collection to road repair, and the loss of important community assets such as libraries, youth centres and women's refuges.

Labour believes in devolving power to local communities but that requires the necessary funding follows. You cannot empower local government if you impoverish it.

A Labour government will give local government extra funding next year. We will initiate a review into reforming council tax and business rates and consider new options such as a land value tax, to ensure local government has sustainable funding for the long term.

Labour is the party of devolution and we believe in handing back power to communities. We will devolve powers over economic development, complete with the necessary funding.

It is through the planning system that communities can shape the kinds of high streets, homes and amenities that they want. But under the Conservatives, planning has been under-resourced and disempowered, with democratic planning authorities unable to stand up to big developers. As a result, planning decisions have become too influenced by narrow economic considerations, with developers' profit taking precedence over community priorities.

A Labour government will properly resource and bolster planning authorities with fuller powers to put people and communities at the heart of planning. We will update compulsory purchase powers to make them more effective as a tool to drive regeneration and unlock planned development.

Under the Conservatives, nearly £400 million has been cut from youth services and over 600 youth centres have closed. Labour will end the cuts to youth services.

We will continue to support all training routes for social workers, including initial social work training provided within or accredited by a higher education institution. We will also prevent the private sector and subsidiaries of private companies from running child protection services. We will deliver earlier protection to victims of abuse by strengthening mandatory reporting, and guaranteeing allegations will be reported and action taken to make children safe.

And we will refocus social care to work with families in local communities to prevent children becoming at risk of going into care.

The government is currently failing to develop a strategy for the wholesale improvement of the care system that delivers for all, not just those children being considered for adoption. We will promote the care and educational achievement of our most vulnerable children and increase support for children in kinship and foster care, and their families. It is important that other forms of care, such as kinship care and fostering, are not marginalised, as this will not result in the step-change we need to see in outcomes for looked after children. Labour will support further regulation of commercial fostering agencies, as well as commissioning a review on establishing a national fostering service.

We will extend Staying Put arrangements to support all children and young people in residential and other forms of care until they are 21.

We will enshrine the European Convention on the Rights of the Child into domestic law.

Labour will fund child burial fees for bereaved parents, ensuring that they are scrapped in all council areas. We recognise that some councils have already made this humane move.

Libraries are vital social assets, valued by communities across the country.

We will ensure libraries are preserved for future generations and updated with wi-fi and computers to meet modern needs. We will reintroduce library standards so that government can assess and guide councils in delivering the best possible service.

Labour will end the closure of Crown Post Office branches, which play a major role in serving their communities. We will also set up a commission to establish a Post Bank, owned by the Post Office and providing a full range of banking services in every community.

Labour will give communities more power to shape their town centres, by strengthening powers to protect post offices, community pharmacies, high street banks, sports clubs, pubs and independent shops, and promote measures to decrease high-street vacancies.

We will set up a national review of local pubs to examine the causes for their large-scale demise, as well as establishing a joint taskforce that will consider future sustainability.

We will reduce the maximum stake on Fixed Odds Betting Terminals from £100 to £2. Labour will also legislate to increase the delay between spins to reduce the addictive nature of the games.

We will give members of the Local Government Pension Scheme full trustee status to help control investments, and reduce fees and charges.

This Conservative government has taken rural communities for granted, with chronic underinvestment in transport, broadband and public services, including the closure of local schools, post offices and libraries.

Rural infrastructure and industry has been neglected. Labour will invest in broadband, housing and transport to create jobs and ensure that the nation's prosperity is felt beyond our large towns and cities.

Labour's national investment plans include coastal protections, better flood management and the broadband and 4G extensions that will underpin the future success of rural small businesses.

Rural councils deliver public services differently, and this needs to be reflected in funding allocation mechanisms. We will consider these differences in our re-evaluation of the business rate schemes.

We will introduce a 'rural-proofing' process so that all our laws, policies and programmes consider their impact on rural communities.

Labour will support tourism at the heart of government. The tourism industry represents 9.6 per cent of UK employment, 4.9 per cent of export and 9 per cent of GDP, but its importance is too often forgotten. Labour will ensure that tourism becomes a national priority again. We will reinstate the cross-Whitehall ministerial group on tourism, and ensure that government ministers across departments understand how their roles fit into the national tourism agenda.

The Conservatives have failed to provide a clear, ambitious or sustainable vision for the future of the farming, food and fishing industries.

We will expand the role of the Groceries Code Adjudicator to ensure suppliers and consumers get a fair deal.

We will reconfigure funds for farming and fishing to support smaller traders, local economies, community benefits and sustainable practices.

We will allow EU workers employed across farming, fishing and food manufacturing to remain in the UK, and reinstate the Seasonal Agricultural Workers Scheme.

We will reinstate the Agricultural Wages Board to underpin employment standards and wages.

We will make utility companies return roads to a condition no worse than when they started digging.

TRANSPORT

Labour will invest in a modern, integrated, accessible and sustainable transport system that is reliable and affordable.

Our transport systems illustrate the abject failure of Tory policies: relentless deregulation, privatisation and fragmentation.

They say we get choice and efficiency but the reality of their transport privatisations has been that services are less reliable, safety is compromised, fares have risen, ticketing has become complicated and air quality has worsened.

On our railways, we pay some of the highest fares in Europe for increasingly unreliable and overcrowded services.

The beneficiaries of public funding siphoned off through transport privatisations have been the earnings of directors, dividends for shareholders and the coffers of overseas governments.

Labour will prioritise public service over private profit. And we will start by bringing our railways back into public ownership, as franchises expire or, in other cases, with franchise reviews or break clauses. We will introduce a Public Ownership of the Railways Bill to repeal the Railways Act 1993 under which the Conservatives privatised our railways.

In public ownership, we will deliver real improvements for passengers by capping fares, introducing free wi-fi across the network, ensuring safe staffing levels, ending the expansion of driver only operations, and introducing legal duties to improve accessibility for people with disabilities.

Across the country we will enable councils to provide first-class bus services by extending the powers to re-regulate local bus services to all areas that want them, and we will support the creation of municipal bus companies that are publicly run for passengers not profit.

Under the Conservatives, bus fares have risen and services have been cut. Labour will introduce regulations to designate and protect routes of critical community value, including those that serve local schools, hospitals and isolated settlements in rural areas.

A publicly owned railway system can be the backbone of our plans for integrated transport. It will be built on the platform of Network Rail, which we will retain whole, working with the devolved administrations. We will ensure new rolling stock is publicly owned and will encourage expansion of public freight services in a publicly owned railway that will leave our roads freer of traffic and our air cleaner. We will facilitate British procurements, including steel, whenever possible.

A Labour government will invest to regenerate the local and regional economies across the whole country, so that every area gets its fair share of transport investment.

A Labour government will complete the HS2 high-speed rail line from London through Birmingham to Leeds and Manchester and then into Scotland, consulting with communities affected about the optimal route. We will link HS2 with other rail investments, such as Crossrail of the North (tying together our great Northern cities) and on to the Durham Freight Centre. We will build a new Brighton Main Line for the South East.

In London, to ensure our capital continues to prosper, we will build Crossrail 2.

To harness the economic potential of new technologies and science, we will complete the Science Vale transport arc that runs from Oxford to Cambridge through Milton Keynes.

And we will deliver rail electrification and expansion across the whole country, including in Wales and the South West. We will also consult with local communities to re-open branch lines.

To prepare for global new trade arrangements, we will study the feasibility of port development across the UK.

We will invest in Scotland, Wales and Northern Ireland too, working with devolved administrations through the UK National Infrastructure Commission and its devolved counterparts.

Our plans will encourage and enable people to get out of their cars, for better health and a cleaner environment.

Labour will position the UK at the forefront of the development, manufacture and use of ultra low emission vehicles, supporting the creation of clean modes of transport through investment in low emission vehicles.

We will retrofit thousands of diesel buses in areas with the most severe air quality problems to Euro 6 standards.

We will reform the legislation governing taxi and private hire services, introducing national standards to guarantee safety and accessibility, updating regulations to keep pace with technological change and ensuring a level playing field between operators.

We will invite the National Infrastructure Commission to recommend the next stages for developing and upgrading the National Cycle Network. We reaffirm the commitments in the Cycling and Walking Investment Strategy.

We will continue to upgrade our highways and improve roadworks at known bottlenecks. The A1 North, the Severn Bridge and the A30 provide essential connections and require our urgent consideration. We will work with the Welsh Government to scrap the tolls on the Severn Bridge.

After seven years of stalled progress, Labour will reset the UK's road safety vision and ambitiously strive for a transport network with zero deaths, reintroducing road-safety targets, setting out bold measures that will continuously improve safety standards.

We will refocus the roads building and maintenance programmes, connecting our communities, feeding public transport hubs and realising untapped economic potential.

Labour recognises the need for additional airport capacity in the South East. We welcome the work done by the Airports Commission, and we will guarantee that any airport expansion adheres to our tests that require noise issues to be addressed, air quality to be protected, the UK's climate change obligations met and growth across the country supported.

We will continue working with our neighbours through the European Union's Highways of the Sea programme and by negotiating to retain membership of the Common Aviation Area and Open Skies arrangements.

ENVIRONMENT

Investing in our environment is investing in our future. We will defend and extend existing environmental protections. We will champion sustainable farming, food and fishing by investing in and promoting skills, technology, market access and innovation.

The Conservatives broke their promise to be the greenest government ever. They have allowed fracking in national parks, evaded their responsibilities on air quality and cut the funding for flood defences. The future of our farming, food and fishing industries hangs in the balance, to be used as leverage in Brexit negotiations.

Only a Labour government will prioritise a sustainable, long-term future for our farming, fishing and food industries, fund robust flood resilience, invest in rural and coastal communities, and guarantee the protection and advancement of environmental quality standards.

The Conservatives' threatened 'bonfire of red tape' is a threat to our environmental protections and to the quality of our lives. Their record on combating climate change and environmental damage has been one of inaction and broken promises.

The balance needs resetting: our air is killing us, our farms face an uncertain future, our fish stocks are collapsing, our oceans are used as dumping grounds, and our forests, green belt, national parks, Areas of Outstanding Natural Beauty and Sites of Special Scientific Interest are all under threat.

Labour will introduce a new Clean Air Act to deal with the Conservative legacy of illegal air quality. We will safeguard habitats and species in the 'blue belts' of the seas and oceans surrounding our island. We will set guiding targets for plastic bottle deposit schemes, working with food manufacturers and retailers to reduce waste. We will protect our bees by prohibiting neonicotinoids as soon as our EU relationship allows us to do so. We will work with farmers and foresters to plant a million trees of native species to promote biodiversity and better flood management. Unlike the Conservatives who attempted to privatise our forests, Labour will keep them in public hands.

Our stewardship of the environment needs to be founded on sound principles and based on scientific assessments. We will establish a science innovation fund, working with farmers and fisheries, that will include support for our small scale fishing fleet.

ANIMAL WELFARE

Animals in our food chain need welfare standards. Domestic animals require stronger protection from cruelty. Wild animals need a sustainable ecosystem.

Labour's vision is for the UK to lead the world with high animal welfare standards in the wild, in farming and for domestic animals. Labour will increase the maximum sentence for those convicted of committing animal cruelty.

We will promote cruelty-free animal husbandry and consult on ways to ensure better enforcement of agreed standards.

We will prohibit the third-party sale of puppies, introduce and enforce a total ban on ivory trading, and support the ban on wild animals in circuses.

We will cease the badger cull, which spreads bovine TB.

Labour ended fox hunting, deer hunting and hare coursing. Only a Labour government will maintain the bans.

CULTURE FOR ALL

Britain's creative industries are the envy of the world, a source of national pride, a driver of inward investment and tourism, and a symbol of the kind of country we are now and aspire to be in the future. As Britain leaves the EU, we will put our world-class creative sector at the heart of our negotiations and future industrial strategy. We need to do more to open up the arts and creative industries to everyone.

We will introduce a £1 billion Cultural Capital Fund to upgrade our existing cultural and creative infrastructure to be ready for the digital age and invest in creative clusters across the country, based on a similar model to enterprise zones. Administered by the Arts Council, the fund will be available over a five-year period. It will be among the biggest arts infrastructure funds ever, transforming the country's cultural landscape.

Labour will maintain free entry to museums and invest in our museums and heritage sector. Conservative cuts to the Arts Council and local authorities have created a very tough financial climate for museums, with some closing or reducing their services, and others starting to charge entry fees. The Cultural Capital Fund will have a particular focus on projects that could increase museums' and galleries' income and viability.

Labour will end cuts to local authority budgets to support the provision of libraries, museums and galleries. We will take steps to widen the reach of the Government Art Collection so that more people can enjoy it.

We will continue to mark the ongoing centenary of the First World War, and the sacrifice of all those who died during it. Labour remains committed to honouring the role of all who have served our country, including the Sikh, Hindu, Muslim and Jewish soldiers who fought for Britain.

Our thriving creative sector, from the games industry to fashion, needs a strong pipeline of skilled talent to sustain its growth.

Labour will introduce an arts pupil premium to every primary school in England – a £160 million annual per year boost for schools to invest in projects that will support cultural activities for schools over the longer term. We will put creativity back at the heart of the curriculum, reviewing the EBacc performance measure to make sure arts are not sidelined from secondary education.

Labour will launch a creative careers advice campaign in schools to demonstrate the range of careers and opportunities available, and the skills required in the creative industries, from the tech sector to theatre production.

Being a performer is a great career. But too often the culture of low or no pay means it isn't an option for those without well-off families to support them. We will work with trade unions and employers to agree sector-specific advice and guidelines on pay and employment standards that will make the sector more accessible to all.

We will improve diversity on and off-screen, working with the film industry and public service and commercial broadcasters to find rapid solutions to improve diversity.

We recognise the serious concern about the 'value gap' between producers of creative content and the digital services that profit from its use, and we will work with all sides to review the way that innovators and artists are rewarded for their work in the digital age.

Music venues play a vital role in supporting the music industry's infrastructure and ensuring a healthy music industry continues in Britain. Labour will review extending the £1,000 pub relief business rates scheme to small music venues.

And we will introduce an 'agent of change' principle in planning law, to ensure that new housing developments can coexist with existing music venues.

We all need to work harder to keep children safe online. Labour will ensure that tech companies are obliged to take measures that further protect children and tackle online abuse. We will ensure that young people understand and are able to easily remove any content they shared on the internet before they turned 18.

MEDIA

The BBC is a national asset which we should all be proud of. Unlike the Conservatives, Labour will always support it and uphold its independence. We will ensure the BBC and public service broadcasting has a healthy future. Labour is committed to keeping Channel 4 in public ownership and will guarantee the future of Welsh-language broadcaster S4C.

Victims of phone hacking have been let down by a Conservative government that promised them justice, but failed to follow through. We will implement the recommendations of part one of the Leveson Inquiry and commence part two which will look into the corporate governance failures that allowed the hacking scandal to occur.

Local newspapers and broadcasting in Britain are an important part of our democracy and culture. We are concerned about closures of local media outlets and the reductions in number of local journalists. Labour will hold a national review local media and into the ownership of national media to ensure plurality.

To protect democracy and media freedom, we will take steps to ensure that Ofcom is better able to safeguard a healthy plurality of media ownership and to put in place clearer rules on who is fit and proper to own or run TV and radio stations.

SPORT

Sport must be run in the interests of those who participate in it and love it, not just for a privileged few. We will give football supporters the opportunity to have a greater say in how their clubs are run. We will legislate for accredited supporters trusts to be able to appoint and remove at least two club directors and to purchase shares when clubs change hands. We will review fan participation in sports governance more widely.

Sporting events must be open and accessible to all. We will push sports authorities to make rapid improvements on access provision for fans with disabilities.

Labour will ensure the Premier League delivers on its promise to invest 5 per cent of its television rights income into the grassroots game to help the next generation of players and coaches, and to improve facilities and pitches. The Premier League has so far failed to do so, despite lucrative new domestic and international TV deals.

The broken ticketing market in the UK means tickets sell out instantly and are put up at vastly inflated prices on ticket-tout websites. Labour will enforce anti-bot legislation and implement the recommendations of the Waterson Review to ensure fair opportunities for fans to buy tickets.

FOR THE MANY NOT THE FEW

CHAPTER 10

EXTENDING DEMOCRACY

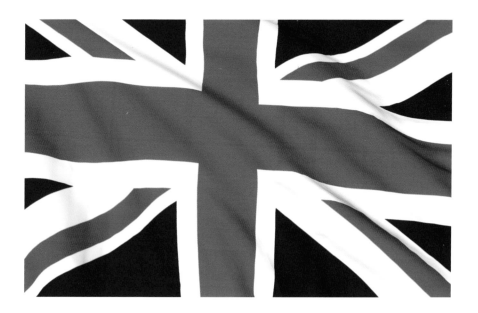

EXTENDING DEMOCRACY

As we change our constitutional relationship with Europe, we must also adjust our own arrangements. Just as many felt that power was too centralised and unaccountable in Brussels, so many feel that about Westminster.

A Labour government will establish a Constitutional Convention to examine and advise on reforming of the way Britain works at a fundamental level.

We will consult on its form and terms of reference and invite recommendations on extending democracy.

This is about where power and sovereignty lies – in politics, the economy, the justice system, and in our communities.

The Convention will look at extending democracy locally, regionally and nationally, considering the option of a more federalised country.

Our fundamental belief is that the Second Chamber should be democratically elected. In the interim period, we will seek to end the hereditary principle and reduce the size of the current House of Lords as part of a wider package of constitutional reform to address the growing democratic deficit across Britain.

We will extend the Freedom of Information Act to private companies that run public services.

We will reduce the voting age to 16. At 16, you are eligible to pay tax, get married or even join the army. You deserve a vote.

We will safeguard our democracy by repealing the Lobbying Act, which has gagged charities, and introduce a tougher statutory register of lobbyists.

ENGLAND

We need a relationship of equals with devolved administrations. Labour will create a role for a Minister for England, who will sit under the Secretary of State for Communities and Local Government, and will work with the Secretaries of State for Scotland, Wales and Northern Ireland.

We will restore regional offices to increase contact between central and local government on the ground.

Labour will be guided by public opinion when determining whether to include directly elected mayors in future devolution deals.

SCOTLAND

Labour opposes a second Scottish independence referendum. It is unwanted and unnecessary, and we will campaign tirelessly to ensure Scotland remains part of the UK. Independence would lead to turbo-charged austerity for Scottish families.

The Scottish Parliament will receive a huge funding increase from our policies, and massive numbers of Scots will benefit from our plans in areas reserved to Westminster.

We will establish a Scottish Investment Bank, with £20 billion of funds available to local projects and Scotland's small businesses, creating work and stimulating the economy.

We will set up an inquiry into blacklisting and will urge the Scottish Government to hold an inquiry into the actions of Scottish police during the miners' strike.

WALES

We are proud of the achievements of the Welsh Labour government and its record of delivery. In government, we will work in partnership to stand up for the people of Wales and protect public services.

We need long-term reform of how the UK allocates public expenditure to ensure that it reflects the needs of different parts of our country and that no nation or region of the UK is unfairly disadvantaged.

We will build on the Development Bank of Wales using more than £10 billion from Labour's new National Investment Bank.

We will bring forward legislation to make the devolution settlement more sustainable as set out by the Welsh Labour government in its Alternative Wales Bill, including the devolution of policing.

NORTHERN
IRELAND

The peace we have today in Northern Ireland is due to the courageous endeavours of those on all sides who have been brave enough to build it.

The Good Friday Agreement, which Labour helped to negotiate, is one of the greatest achievements of Labour in office.

We will continue to fully support the principles and structures inherent within the Good Friday Agreement and we remain committed to working with all sides to deliver real peace and greater prosperity to Northern Ireland.

CHAPTER 11

A MORE
EQUAL SOCIETY

A MORE EQUAL SOCIETY

The Labour Party is the party of equality and seeks to build a society and world free from all forms of racism, anti-Semitism and Islamophobia. Labour has a strong record on progressing women's rights and freedoms that we can be proud of.

Labour brought in the Equal Pay Act, the Sex Discrimination Act, the Equality Act, the Minimum Wage and introduced Sure Start. Every progressive piece of equality legislation has been delivered by Labour.

Under the Conservatives, progress is being rolled back for women, people with disabilities, LGBT people and BAME communities. Cuts to public services and social security are landing disproportionately on women and ethnic minorities, with 86 per cent of the money raised from the Tories' tax and social security changes coming from women's pockets.

It was a Labour government that enshrined the rights and freedoms contained in the European Convention on Human Rights into UK law, marking the birth of the Human Rights Act.

Devastating cuts to the Equality and Human Rights Commission by the Conservatives reveal their real attitude, beyond the rhetoric, to issues of equality and discrimination. These cuts have been made amid the rise in hate crime recorded by the police in the last year. A Labour government will enhance the powers and functions of this commission, making it truly independent, to ensure it can support ordinary working people to effectively challenge any discrimination they may face. A Labour government will reinstate the public sector equality duties and seek to extend them to the private sector, ensuring all citizens benefit from this Labour legislation.

WOMEN

The advances for women in Britain and around the world have been fought and won by determined women working together for real change, often in the face of resistance and even abuse.

Labour has a proud record on progressing women's rights and freedoms. We brought in the Equal Pay Act, the Sex Discrimination Act, the Equality Act, the Minimum Wage and introduced Sure Start. Ours will be a government for women, with a cabinet of at least 50 per cent women, which fights inequality and misogyny in every part of society.

A Labour government will gender audit all policy and legislation for its impact on women before implementation.

Labour will continue to ensure a woman's right to choose a safe, legal abortion – and we will work with the Assembly to extend that right to women in Northern Ireland.

Violence against women and girls continues to be a global epidemic, affecting an estimated one in three women worldwide. In the UK, on average two women are killed by their current or a former partner every week. Under the Conservatives, over a third of all local authority funding to domestic and sexual violence services was already cut by 2012.

Labour will appoint a new commissioner to enforce minimum standards in tackling domestic and sexual violence. A Violence Against Women Commissioner would also provide stable central funding for women's refuges and rape crisis centres and encourage sharing of best practice between local authorities.

Maternity discrimination under the Conservatives is out of control, almost doubling in the past ten years. Many mothers are reluctant to raise complaints about discrimination and unfair treatment. Unlawful maternity and pregnancy discrimination is now more common in Britain's workplaces than ever before, with 54,000 pregnant women and new mothers forced out of their jobs in 2015. Labour will reverse the unfair employment tribunal fees which literally price people out of justice. Labour will also extend the time period for applying for maternity discrimination to the employment tribunal from three to six months.

Labour will work with the Health and Safety Executive to make mandatory a workplace risk assessment for pregnant women so necessary adaptions can be made, and review support for women who have miscarriages.

LGBT EQUALITY

Labour has a proud record of championing the fight for LGBT equality. We abolished Section 28, equalised the age of consent, created civil partnerships, and it was only through Labour votes that equal marriage became law. However, there is still a long way to go on issues such as education, equal access to public services, levels of LGBT hate crime, and mental and physical wellbeing.

A Labour government will reform the Gender Recognition Act and the Equality Act 2010 to ensure they protect Trans people by changing the protected characteristic of 'gender assignment' to 'gender identity' and remove other outdated language such as 'transsexual'.

Labour will bring the law on LGBT hate crimes into line with hate crimes based on race and faith, by making them aggravated offences.

To tackle bullying of LGBT young people, Labour will ensure that all teachers receive initial and ongoing training on the issues students face and how to address them. And we will ensure that the new guidance for relationships and sex education is LGBT inclusive.

Likewise, we will ensure all frontline health and social care professionals receive ongoing training to understand and meet the needs of LGBT patients and service users. Labour will ensure that NHS England completes the trial programme to provide PrEP as quickly as possible, and fully roll out the treatment to high-risk groups to help reduce HIV infection.

DIVERSE COMMUNITIES

Now more than ever, we need to celebrate the profound and enriching transformation brought by the diversity of people in this country, with all their different experiences, talents and contributions.

Today Black and Asian-owned businesses are an important and growing feature of our economy and society. These businesses are important not just because of their financial contribution; they have also helped transform particular sectors of the economy.

The Labour Party is the party of equality. We seek to build a society free from all forms of racism, anti-Semitism and Islamophobia.

We should all be deeply troubled by the rise in racially aggravated attacks and race hate crime in the past year. Anti-Semitic incidents are also on the rise once more and we are committed to combatting this trend with adequate resources and firm political will.

Commissioning a report on our own party was an unprecedented step in British politics, demonstrating a commitment to tackling prejudice wherever it is found. Labour is already acting on recommendations, including reform of internal disciplinary procedures to make them firmer and fairer, and expansion of training to tackle anti-Semitism. On a matter of such importance, Labour urges all democratic political parties to do the same.

We will end racism and discrimination against Gypsy, Roma and Traveller communities, and protect the right to lead a nomadic way of life.

Black and Asian workers still suffer a massive pay gap. By introducing equal pay audit requirements on large employers, Labour will close this pay gap. By making the Minimum Wage a real Living Wage, we will benefit ethnic minority workers who are more likely to be on low pay.

We will implement the Parker Review recommendations to increase ethnic diversity on the boards of Britain's largest companies.

PEOPLE WITH DISABILITIES

Over the last seven years people with disabilities have been failed by the Conservative government.

People with disabilities have been vilified with divisive rhetoric like 'scroungers' and 'shirkers'. In this climate, recorded disability hate crime has increased.

Last year the UN published a report concluding that the Conservative government had committed "grave, systematic violations of the rights of persons with disabilities".

Currently 4.2 million People with disabilities live in poverty in Britain, and the disability employment gap remains stubbornly high.

Labour believes in the social model of disability – that it is society which disables people, and it is our job to remove those barriers. The previous Labour government signed the UN Convention on the Rights of Persons with Disabilities (UNCRPD). The next Labour government will sign the UNCRPD into UK law.

Labour will act to tackle discrimination, remove barriers and ensure social security delivers dignity and empowerment, not isolation and stigma. Labour will legislate to make terminal illness a protected characteristic under the Equality Act.

Autism covers a wide range of conditions that reflect neurological differences among people. We will work with employers, trade unions and public services to improve awareness of neurodiversity in the workplace and in society.

Labour will give British Sign Language full recognition as a recognised language.

CHAPTER 12

A GLOBAL BRITAIN

A GLOBAL BRITAIN

Labour will take all necessary measures to protect the security of our citizens and country. We will put conflict resolution and human rights at the heart of foreign policy, commit to working through the UN, end support for unilateral aggressive wars of intervention and back effective action to alleviate the refugee crisis.

Unlike the Conservatives, Labour believes Britain's foreign policy should be guided by the values of peace, universal rights and international law. Today, these values are being tested. As we leave the European Union, keeping Britain global is one of our country's most urgent tasks.

We face the most complex, interwoven security and development challenges of our time; ongoing wars across the Middle East, unprecedented numbers of refugees, global terrorism, climate change, the threat of nuclear conflict, a devastating food crisis across East Africa and beyond, an erratic US administration and a more combative government in Russia.

The lessons of the past, including those from the Chilcot Inquiry, show why our response to these challenges must be different. We cannot seek to solve the world's problems on our own, but instead must exhaust diplomatic solutions alongside international, regional and local partners within the framework of international law.

This will require a modern and inclusive strategy, uniting the interwoven foreign policy instruments of diplomacy, defence and development.

DIPLOMACY

Labour recognises that, in leaving the EU, Britain will face both challenges and opportunities. We are deeply ambitious for our country's future and will draw on our international networks to make Britain a champion of multilateral engagement. We will invest in the UK's diplomatic services, rebuilding some of the key capabilities lost as a result of Tory cuts.

Since the Second World War, Britain's most important diplomatic relationship has been with the US. But that special relationship is based on shared values. When the current Trump administration chooses to ignore them, whether by discriminating on the basis of religion or breaking its climate change commitments, we will not be afraid to disagree.

From the Middle East to Africa, in recent years millions of people have been killed, injured or displaced through wars, terrorism and military intervention. In Syria alone, more than 400,000 people have been killed. Labour will work tirelessly to end the conflict and get the diplomatic process back on track, while fully supporting international efforts to investigate, prosecute and convict the perpetrators of war crimes.

Labour is strongly committed to reducing human suffering caused by war. We will publish a strategy for protecting civilians in conflict, setting out detailed plans for work on conflict prevention and resolution, post-conflict peacebuilding, and justice for the victims of war crimes. Labour has created a Minister for Peace and Disarmament to lead this work.

Labour is committed to a comprehensive peace in the Middle East based on a two-state solution – a secure Israel alongside a secure and viable state of Palestine. There can be no military solution to this conflict and all sides must avoid taking action that would make peace harder to achieve. That means both an end to the blockade, occupation and settlements, and an end to rocket and terror attacks. Labour will continue to press for an immediate return to meaningful negotiations leading to a diplomatic resolution. A Labour government will immediately recognise the state of Palestine.

We will also urge negotiations towards a political resolution in all other regions currently experiencing conflict, including Kashmir, Libya, Nigeria, Sudan, South Sudan, Somalia and Yemen, and give our strong support to those countries already working to end decades of division, including Colombia, Cyprus and the Democratic Republic of Congo.

In other regions, including the Korean Peninsula and the South China Sea, rising tensions threaten global peace. Under a Labour government, Britain will work to reduce those tensions through an insistence on multilateral political dialogue.

From Afghanistan and Iraq to the streets of European cities, Daesh continues to commit acts of indiscriminate barbarism. We will take all lawful action necessary to counter and confront this evil, and we will advocate a long-term multinational political strategy, led by regional actors, to tackle the spread of extremism.

In our discussions with different governments, including China, Egypt, the Gulf States, Myanmar, the Philippines, Russia and Turkey, we will urge respect for human rights and the rule of law. We will review all training and equipment contracts with repressive regimes, to ensure that Britain never colludes in the mistreatment of civilians.

We will always stand up for the rights, interests and self-determination of Britain's overseas territories and their citizens, whether protecting the sovereignty of the Falkland Islands against anyone who would seek to challenge it, or supporting the right of the Chagos islanders to return to their homelands.

We will reclaim Britain's leading role in tackling climate change, working hard to preserve the Paris Agreement and deliver on international commitments to reduce emissions while mitigating the impacts of climate change on developing countries.

While strengthening our commitment to the UN, we also acknowledge its shortcomings, particularly in light of repeated abuses of the veto power by some permanent members of the UN Security Council. We will work with our international partners to build support for UN reform and make its institutions more effective and responsive. We will appoint dedicated global ambassadors for women's rights, LGBT rights and religious freedom to fight discrimination and promote equality globally.

Exports, trade and investment play a vital role in creating jobs and growth in Britain, and Labour supports the considerable contribution that a responsible, world-leading defence and security industry makes to the UK economy. However, we also believe that strong export controls have a vital role to play in sustaining a legitimate trade in arms, while protecting UK jobs and R&D. Labour will therefore implement the Arms Trade Treaty to a consistently high standard, including ceasing arms exports to countries where there is concern that they will be used to violate international humanitarian law (IHL).

In particular, Labour will demand a comprehensive, independent, UN-led investigation into alleged violations of IHL in Yemen, including air strikes on civilians by the Saudi-led coalition. We will immediately suspend any further arms sales for use in the conflict until that investigation is concluded.

Labour remains committed to an independent inquiry into Britain's military role in the 1984 raid on the Golden Temple in Amritsar.

DEFENCE

The primary duty of any government is to protect and defend its citizens. We live in a period of growing international tensions. A strong, viable and sustainable defence and security policy must be strategic and evidence led.

As previous incoming governments have done, a Labour government will order a complete strategic defence and security review when it comes into office, to assess the emerging threats facing Britain, including hybrid and cyber warfare. Cyber security will form an integral part of our defence and security strategy and we will introduce a cyber-security charter for companies working with the Ministry of Defence.

We will ensure that our armed forces are properly equipped and resourced to respond to wide-ranging security challenges. Labour will commit to effective UN peacekeeping, including support for a UN Emergency Peace Service.

As the security threats and challenges we face are not bound by geographic borders, it is vital that as Britain leaves the EU, we maintain our close relationship with our European partners. Alongside our commitment to NATO, we will continue to work with the EU on a range of operational missions to promote and support global and regional security.

The last Labour government consistently spent above the NATO benchmark of 2 per cent of GDP. Conservative spending cuts have put Britain's security at risk, shrinking the army to its smallest size since the Napoleonic wars. The scrapping of Nimrod, HMS Ark Royal and the Harrier jump-jets have weakened our defences and cost British taxpayers millions.

Labour's commitment to spending at least 2 per cent of GDP on defence will guarantee that our Armed Forces have the necessary capabilities to fulfil the full range of obligations, and ensure our conventional forces are versatile and able to deploy in a range of roles.

Labour supports the renewal of the Trident nuclear deterrent. As a nuclear-armed power, our country has a responsibility to fulfil our obligations under the Nuclear Non-Proliferation Treaty. Labour will lead multilateral efforts with international partners and the UN to create a nuclear-free world.

The UK defence industry is world-leading, and Labour will continue to support development and innovation in this sector and to ensure that it can continue to rely on a highly skilled workforce. We are committed to a procurement process that supports the British steel industry and defence manufacturing industry, which in turn provide good jobs throughout the supply chain. Labour will publish a Defence Industrial Strategy White Paper, including a National Shipbuilding Strategy to secure a long-term future for the industry, workers and UK defence.

We have a duty to properly reward and remunerate our Armed Forces. Under the Conservatives, our Armed Forces have been hit by rent rises, pay restraint, and changes to tax and benefits, putting real pressure on service personnel and their families. We will ensure they get the pay and living conditions that their service merits.

Dedicated service personnel are at the heart of our defence policy. Labour will immediately examine recruitment and retention policies in order to stem the exodus seen under the Conservatives. We will publish new strategic equality objectives to ensure our personnel reflect our diverse society.

We will drive up standards in Service Accommodation, and take action where private companies have failed to deliver. We will consult with service personnel, giving them greater autonomy over their housing choices, and review and improve the Forces Help to Buy scheme.

Personnel who are injured while serving should have prompt access to support and compensation. We will resist any Conservative proposals to abolish the right to seek legal redress against the MoD where compensation claims cannot be otherwise settled.

We are fully committed to supporting our veterans. We will promote greater awareness of the Armed Forces Covenant, seek greater consistency in its implementation by public authorities, and promote increased participation in the Corporate Covenant.

We will also roll out a Homes Fit for Heroes programme that will insulate the homes of disabled veterans for free.

DEVELOPMENT

Labour has a proud record on international development. We will continue to spend 0.7 per cent of gross national income on official development assistance, and develop a targeted development agenda based on the principles of redistribution, social justice, women's rights and poverty reduction.

Labour will take robust action to end the self-regulation of Department for International Development private contractors, establishing and enforcing new rules to ensure aid is used to reduce poverty for the many, not to increase profits for the few.

We fully support the Sustainable Development Goals (SDGs) agreed globally to eradicate poverty and protect the environment. Labour will develop a cross-government strategy for ensuring the SDGs are implemented, and report annually to Parliament on our performance.

In the wake of Brexit, to fulfil our national obligations under the SDGs, Labour will guarantee the least developed countries continued access to the UK market to protect vital export revenues.

There are more refugees and displaced people around the world than at any time since the Second World War. This is a failure of diplomacy, conflict

resolution and of human rights, which is why they will be at the heart of Labour's foreign policy.

The Conservatives have completely failed to show any leadership on this issue. In the first 100 days of government, we will produce a cross-departmental strategy to meet our international obligations on the refugee crisis.

The current global tax system is deeply unjust. Africa's economies alone lose more than £46 billion annually through corruption and tax evasion – more than 10 times what they receive in aid. Labour will act decisively on tax havens, introducing strict standards of transparency for crown dependencies and overseas territories, including a public register of owners, directors, major shareholders and beneficial owners for all companies and trusts.

We will work in partnership with communities in the Global South to develop long-term strategies for strengthening economies and societies. We would reinstate the Civil Society Challenge Fund to support trade unions, women's associations and other civil society organisations which are the most effective forces in winning human rights and workers' rights.

Jobs in global supply chains can be of enormous importance to working people across the Global

South, but human rights abuses and exploitation of lower environmental standards and workers' rights are too common. Labour is committed to ensuring respect for human rights, workers' rights and environmental sustainability in the operations of British businesses around the world, and we will work to tighten the rules governing corporate accountability for abuses in global supply chains.

Labour will work with business to ensure the provisions of the Modern Slavery Act are fully respected, including reporting on due diligence in supply chains. We will extend the remit of the Groceries Code Adjudicator beyond direct suppliers to ensure fair treatment for all those producing goods for the UK's largest supermarkets.

At least a billion people around the world cannot currently obtain the health services they need, and another 100 million are pushed below the poverty line as a result of paying for their services. We will establish a Centre for Universal Health Coverage, providing global partnerships, support and encouragement to countries that want UHC, helping them to generate the funding and systems required for its delivery.

We will invest in new public-health driven research and development to find effective and affordable treatments for diseases in the developing world, including fighting TB, malaria, HIV/AIDS and neglected tropical diseases.